Sheila Rogers
Acts 26:18

I BELIEVE IN GOD, SO I'M SAVED, RIGHT?

SHEILA STAFFORD ROGERS

Published by Innovo Publishing, LLC
www.innovopublishing.com
1-888-546-2111

Publishing Books, eBooks, Audiobooks, Music, Screenplays, & Courses for the Christian & wholesome markets since 2008.

**I BELIEVE IN GOD,
SO I'M SAVED, RIGHT?**

Copyright © 2023 by Sheila S. Rogers
All rights reserved.

No part of this publication may be reproduced, stored in a retrieval system, or transmitted in any form or by any means electronic, mechanical, photocopying, recording, or otherwise, without the prior written permission of the Author.

Unless otherwise noted, all scripture is taken from the *Holy Bible*, New Living Translation, copyright © 1996, 2004, 2015 by Tyndale House Foundation. Used by permission of Tyndale House Publishers, Inc., Carol Stream, Illinois 60188. All rights reserved.

Scripture marked "ASV" was taken from the American Standard Version of the Bible. Public domain.

Scripture marked "CSB" was taken from The Christian Standard Bible. Copyright © 2017 by Holman Bible Publishers. Used by permission. Christian Standard Bible®, and CSB® are federally registered trademarks of Holman Bible Publishers, all rights reserved.

Scripture marked "ESV" was taken from The Holy Bible, English Standard Version. ESV® Text Edition: 2016. Copyright © 2001 by Crossway Bibles, a publishing ministry of Good News Publishers.

Scripture marked "KJV" was taken from the King James Version of the Bible. Public domain.

Scripture marked "NASB" was taken from the New American Standard Bible®, Copyright © 1960, 1971, 1977, 1995, 2020 by The Lockman Foundation. All rights reserved.

Scripture marked "NIV" was taken from the Holy Bible, New International Version®, NIV® Copyright ©1973, 1978, 1984, 2011 by Biblica, Inc.® Used by permission. All rights reserved worldwide.

Scripture marked "NKJV" was taken from the New King James Version®. Copyright © 1982 by Thomas Nelson. Used by permission. All rights reserved.

Scripture marked "TLB" was taken from The Living Bible copyright © 1971 by Tyndale House Foundation. Used by permission of Tyndale House Publishers Inc., Carol Stream, Illinois 60188. All rights reserved.

Scripture marked "VOICE" was taken from The Voice Bible Copyright © 2012 Thomas Nelson, Inc. The Voice™ translation © 2012 Ecclesia Bible Society All rights reserved.

Library of Congress Control Number: 2023910570
ISBN: 978-1-61314-926-3

Cover Design & Interior Layout: Innovo Publishing, LLC
Printed in the United States of America
U.S. Printing History
First Edition: 2023

Has God called you to create a Christ-centered or wholesome book, eBook, audiobook, music album, screenplay, or online course? Visit Innovo's educational center (cpportal.com) to learn how to accomplish your calling with excellence.

To Allen, my wonderfully patient husband, who from day one encouraged me to step into the unknown under the leading of the Holy Spirit. Who selflessly, untiringly, and at all hours listened, read, and cheered me on. I love you.

CONTENTS

Preface ix
Introduction xi

CHAPTER 1: Believe 15

CHAPTER 2: Prayer 31

CHAPTER 3: Testimony 43

CHAPTER 4: Repentance 51

CHAPTER 5: Works and Good Fruit 57

CHAPTER 6: Obedience 65

CHAPTER 7: The Holy Word of God: The Bible 75

CHAPTER 8: Worship 85

CHAPTER 9: Personal Relationship 93

CHAPTER 10: Love 105

CHAPTER 11: Witness 117

CHAPTER 12: End Times 131

CHAPTER 13: Conclusion 137

Afterword: The Road to Salvation 141

PREFACE

*I believe in God,
so I'm saved, right?*

This simple statement coupled with that simple question is like the proverbial onion with many layers. That's why I was convicted to write about this subject in depth. This has been an accepted thought among the masses for far too long, and unless they are shown the truth of the Bible, their eternity will be a dismal one. The fact that so many people I know and love have this very lethal mindset compels me to bring to light what the Bible has to say about this very thing.

God's Word is to always be our standard by which we determine fact from fiction. It has so distressed me through the years to see people claiming to be Christians just because they believe in God, and yet there is no evidence of that claim seen in their life. There is simply no fruit to back up their faulty belief. It's my sincere desire to, as Acts 26:18 says, "Open their eyes that they may turn from darkness to light, from the power of Satan to God. Then they will receive forgiveness for their sins and be given a place among God's people set apart by their faith in Me."

How many times have I prayed that prayer over the names of people I know and love and even those who are strangers to me? With God as my guide and my wisdom, it is my prayer that this book, through the power of God's Holy Spirit, will cause the scales to fall from those blind eyes that they may really know God.

INTRODUCTION

I believe in God.

"I believe in God." This statement is fast becoming outdated in these last days, as I believe we are now in. It is painfully clear with each passing year that Satan is gaining a strong foothold in our world. But know this: Satan can only do as God will allow. This has always been true. God's sovereignty is expressed throughout the scriptures. Job 42:1-2 says, "Then Job replied to the Lord: I know that You can do anything, and no one can stop You." Psalm 103:19 declares, "The Lord has made the heavens His throne; from there He rules over everything." His divine will, will always be accomplished.

So, as many voices as we hear denying God's existence (as I just minutes ago read that Britney Spears announced she no longer believes in God), there is a vast number of well-meaning but blinded people proclaiming that they are indeed saved, are children of God, are Christians, because they "believe in God." They are as sincere as anyone can be, yet they have an incomplete understanding of the gospel. To illustrate this, let me share a story told to a church by a pastor I knew. He began by saying he was traveling by plane somewhere and had just boarded. He had his ticket in hand and quickly found his assigned seat. As he was settling in, another man boarding the plane politely informed him he was in the wrong seat. He explained, no, he was in the correct seat. He had checked the number, and it was definitely the right one. The man was insistent that there had been a mistake and was not leaving until he was in *his* seat. The pastor was beginning to get a bit annoyed with his interrogation when the man asked to see his ticket. He confidently handed it over, knowing this would

INTRODUCTION

put an end to the misunderstanding. However, the man said, "Sir, you are definitely in the right seat. You're just on the wrong plane!" As embarrassing as that was, the pastor learned a huge life lesson, which is this: you can *sincerely* believe in something and still be wrong. Sincerity doesn't automatically mean that what you believe is true.

> You can *sincerely* believe in something and still be wrong. Sincerity doesn't automatically mean that what you believe is true.

Second Corinthians 4:4 says, "Satan, who is the god of this world, has blinded the minds of those who don't believe. They are unable to see the glorious light of the Good News. They don't understand this message about the glory of Christ, who is the exact likeness of God." Since they are at a disadvantage and cannot understand spiritually, Satan has tossed in twists and turns to distort their understanding of the truth of God. What scripture says has been muddied up in translation. So they embrace what *sounds* like truth. It's here where Satan ties their hands behind their backs, making them hostages to human reasoning and false arguments. He has used this delusional "I believe in God" way of thinking as a super weapon to capture people into having a *form* of godliness. Satan has convinced them they are saved. So it's no wonder that when they are asked to give witness of their *belief* in God, they are not sure what that means. They feel as if they are being challenged and will often accuse Christians of being judgmental of their faith, not realizing, had they read the Bible, that God calls Christians to have a righteous judgment and godly discernment (John 7:24 CSB). Christians are called to judge righteously with the love of Christ empowering them. If a parent never "judged" the wrong behavior of their children, we would assume they cared very little for them. God loves everyone with an everlasting love and will do whatever it takes to bring a precious soul to a place of repentance resulting in salvation.

What more does God have to do to prove His love for us than giving His one and only Son to be crucified for our sins?

INTRODUCTION

Oswald Chambers shared this amazing truth in regard to God's love for us and our salvation:

> Never build your case for forgiveness on the idea that God is our Father and He will forgive us *because He loves us*. That contradicts the revealed truth of God in Jesus Christ. It makes the Cross unnecessary and the redemption "much ado about nothing." God forgives sin *only* because of the death of Christ. God could forgive people in no other way than by the death of His Son, and Jesus is exalted as Savior because of His death.[1]

Yes, God loves everyone, and it is because of that love He made a way for us to be forgiven. That way is Jesus.

As I begin this journey to expose what *true belief* in Jesus Christ looks like, I wish to add that my intention in writing this book is to leave no stone unturned. I hope to uproot wrong theology. I want to spotlight several words and dig as deeply as I can to uncover perhaps that one truth that will penetrate the unbelieving heart, or should I say, the heart that mistakenly believes it is saved. It is through God's Holy Spirit that I hope to accomplish this very thing.

It's also my prayer as you read these pages that you'll take time to digest what is written about these certain words and what they really mean from God's perspective so that by the time you turn to the last page, you'll have a clearer understanding about where you stand with God and whether your salvation is authentic or not. I'm praying that your eyes will be open to His truth that you need to see and that you will set your life on an entirely different course—one that leads to genuine salvation and life eternal.

---

1. Oswald Chambers, *My Utmost for His Highest*, from devotional dated November 21 entitled "It Is Finished," updated edition, edited by James Reimann (Discovery House from our Daily Bread Ministries, authorized by the Oswald Chambers Publications Assoc., Ltd., 1992), emphasis added.

INTRODUCTION

Following is a list of words that hopefully I can give clarity to and, by so doing, give you something to chew on and pray over, asking God to give you genuine understanding of what characterizes true salvation. May God bless you as you begin in earnest your quest to really know Him.

Believe
Prayer
Testimony
Repentance
Works and Fruit
Obedience
God's Word
Worship
Personal Relationship
Love
Witness
End Times

May I suggest, as a way to examine your heart to see whether you do indeed belong to Christ or not, that you underline or highlight words, phrases, or sentences that seem to jump off the page at you. These may be words specifically anointed by God Himself to bring your heart into alignment with His will for you. Words that may ultimately be life changing.

I have included several personal stories within these chapters that underscore the relevance of some of the featured words. I hope to give you a mental picture of how these selected words come alive as we *literally* live them out for Christ.

Let this verse be our cornerstone as we diligently look for the truth about our salvation: "Examine yourselves to see if your faith is genuine. Test yourselves" (2 Cor 13:5a).

Chapter 1

BELIEVE

*They replied, "Believe in the Lord Jesus, and you will be saved—
you and your household."
—Acts 16:31 (NIV)*

Since this is the word that is being questioned or challenged, let's begin with an accurate understanding of its meaning. Let's read a few verses from the Bible that mention the word *believe*.

> *For I am not ashamed of the gospel, for it is the power of God for salvation to everyone who believes, to the Jew first and also to the Greek. (Rom. 1:16 ESV)*

> *But to all who believed Him and accepted Him, He gave the right to become children of God. (John 1:12)*

> *Jesus told her, "I am the resurrection and the life. Anyone who believes in me will live, even after dying. Everyone who lives in me and believes in me will never ever die." (John 11:25-26a)*

I BELIEVE IN GOD, SO I'M SAVED, RIGHT?

For God loved the world so much that He gave His only Son, so that anyone who believes in Him shall not perish but have eternal life. (John 3:16 TLB)

There is no shortage of scripture telling us that "believing in Jesus" is our way to salvation. And quite honestly, it seems that among my peers, we so often experienced what has been labeled, "easy believism." This has been one of the most devastating mistakes in our evangelical church. However well it was intended, it has become a millstone around the necks of many.

Has this ever been your experience? You've just listened to a wonderful message from God's Word. The preacher then asks, "It's time you made a decision concerning your eternity. Do you want to go to heaven or hell?" Well, of course no one wants to go to hell! No one, not even the toughest hombre, would ever say they'd enjoy living out their eternity in fire and brimstone. Then he goes on to ask, "Do you believe Jesus is God's Son and that He was crucified, died, and rose again?" Well, that sounds like your Easter lessons, doesn't it? Yes, of course you believe those things. Our Sunday school teachers wouldn't lie to us. He concludes with this death-sentence statement: "Then pray this prayer." Of course this is the Sinner's Prayer he's referring to. But one must *want* Jesus to be their Lord and Savior for it to have any merit. Nevertheless, many want *heaven* more than *Jesus*, so they repeat what they've been told to say. I can almost hear the blade of the guillotine as it falls and with it a near *guarantee* you'll live the rest of your life believing that you just got saved! No number of well-meaning friends is going to make you believe otherwise. After all, you prayed the prayer! But Pastor Adrian Rogers once said, "You can't use a prayer as a smokescreen to keep you from repentance."[2]

What does the word *believe* mean in Greek, its original language? *Pisteuo* means to be convinced that something is trustworthy and factual. However, being convinced of facts, such

---

2. Adrian Rogers, *Adrianisms: The Wit and Wisdom of Adrian Rogers* (Memphis, TN: Love Worth Finding Ministries, 2006), 45.

as Christ's crucifixion, is not enough to gain salvation. Why not? Because the kind of belief needed for salvation, as John 3:16 says, must be a personal belief, an investment of your life, a deliberate and intentional turning over of the rights to your life to Christ. Not only did Jesus Christ die on the cross, but He died on the cross for *my* sins, being a substitutionary sacrifice to God on my behalf. We must believe that the One who knew no sin became sin to save *me*. That's much more than just believing facts.

Believe also means "trust" in Greek. Anyone who wants to be saved must trust that it is Christ alone who saves us. It's not being good or giving money to the church. It's not baptism or singing in the choir. It's not memorizing scripture (Satan did that also—Matt. 4:6) or learning the Ten Commandments. It's not going on mission trips or teaching a Sunday school class. It's not having cute farmhouse scripture signs all over your house. In fact, it's not *doing* anything. Jesus Christ is our only way of salvation. He's already done everything that is required for us to be saved. John 14:6 says, "Jesus told him, 'I am the Way, the Truth, and the Life. No one can come to the Father except through Me.'" So again, we see the importance of understanding what belief in God really means since that is the only way to God.

There is a difference in believing in the factual existence of something and believing *in* something where you're relinquishing the rights to your life. The first way is agreement that something exists and that there are facts to support it. The other way is a total investment, a surrender of yourself, your heart, your soul, making it your identity. For example, I believe in the existence of molecules even though I can't see them. But I don't believe *in* them to the extent I would bend a knee to them in reverence or surrender my life in obedience to them! My everyday thoughts and actions do not revolve around pleasing them. I don't plan the course of my days on the fact that molecules exist. I haven't claimed molecules as my personal identity and reason for getting up in the mornings. So it is apparent that the word *believe* has more than one meaning. Since it does, it is absolutely imperative we understand which one is used in John 3:16, the one that is essential for eternal life. "For God loved the world so much that He gave His one and only Son, so that everyone who *believes* in Him will not perish but have eternal life" (emphasis added).

Romans 10:9-10 says, "If you openly declare that Jesus is Lord and *believe* in your heart that God raised him from the dead, you will be saved. For it is by believing in your heart that you are made right with God, and it is by openly declaring your faith that you are saved" (emphasis added). There are few, if any, who, having just an intellectual knowledge of Jesus, would then set about confessing to their circle of friends and strangers alike that Jesus is the only way to salvation or that Jesus transformed their life. This is because they are not personally identifying with Christ. True faith or belief that leads to salvation is something much different. I have had strained conversations with individuals who will look me squarely in the eye after hearing a message preached and comment on what they've just heard. They are convinced they've understood rightly, yet their comments are sadly off because they are incapable of seeing or understanding what is spiritual. Until our spiritual eyes are open to see the Word, it's like drilling for oil that's found deep in the ground but only scraping away at the top soil, the part that can be visibly seen. These dear individuals understand God's Word purely from a worldly or intelligent view. They, without realizing it, give only an intellectual dissection of the scriptures, which is not the way the Word is to be read or understood. The words are getting into their heads, and they try their best to assimilate them in their brains. But the problem is, it's not our *brain* that needs to change. It's our *heart*. First Corinthians 2:14 (ESV) says, "The natural person does not accept the things of the Spirit of God, for they are folly to him, and he's not able to understand them because they are spiritually discerned."

> Until our spiritual eyes are open to see the Word, it's like drilling for oil that's found deep in the ground but only scraping away at the top soil, the part that can be visibly seen.

True belief in Jesus Christ is a full-on commitment to the only hope humanity has. It doesn't make sense to wave a banner for one thing then live your life in opposition to that banner. One or the other is a lie. Genuine belief in Jesus Christ is a surrendered life of obedience wrapped in gratitude and love to the One who died for you. So what is meant by a *surrendered life*? Ask yourself what are the components of your life that make you who you are. What are the puzzle pieces of your life that come together to form the essence of you? Consider these areas of our lives: our careers or jobs, our finances, our friends and family, our recreation and entertainment, our love life, our personal and spiritual development, and our environment. God demands that we give Him every area of our life. But what does that mean? This can be answered this way:

> Surrender is a battle term. It implies giving up all rights to the conqueror. When an opposing army surrenders, they lay down their arms, and the winner takes control from then on. Surrendering to God works the same way. God has a plan for our lives, and surrendering to Him means we set aside our *own* plans and eagerly seek His. The good news is that God's plan for us is *always* in our best interest unlike our own plans that often lead to destruction. Our Lord is a wise and beneficent victor; He conquers us to bless us.[3]

There are innumerable pieces to the puzzle that is *us*. But sometimes we may be reluctant to hand it all over to God. After all, we'd still like to have a little control over what happens in our own lives. We want to claim ownership of snippets of our lives. God can have everything *except* my love life or my finances or what career I choose or even my addictions.

---

3. GotQuestions.org, "What does it mean to surrender to God?" (January 4, 2022).

But just know that whatever we claim for ourselves becomes a veil obscuring God from our view. What I don't absolutely surrender and give up to God comes between God and me. Once I put everything on the altar and leave it there, the brightness of God's smiling face will be seen. I think after Abraham relinquished any claim he had on Isaac, he looked at the world in a very different fashion. What you hang on to will weigh you down and hinder you in your pursuit of spiritual perfection.[4]

God demands our totality, our entire selves, because His Son gave His totality on the cross so we might have eternal life. When we live a life surrendered to Christ, there are no puzzle pieces that we can hide away or hold back at our discretion. Certainly as our faith grows, there will be areas of our life that we will become convicted about and that we've not fully entrusted to God. We should always be in a state of growth in our Christian life, learning how to trust God more with all the areas of it. But don't be deceived! To know there are areas in our lives that we've not yet turned over to Christ's authority and to willingly withhold what is rightfully God's is disobedience. Yet if we prayerfully come to Christ repenting, He will surely forgive us. Jesus Christ didn't just partially die on the cross. He wasn't just slightly mutilated by the scourging. He gave His all. Jesus said in Matthew 22:37, "You must love the Lord your God with *all* your heart, *all* your soul, and *all* your mind" (emphasis added). That sums up our totality.

You may reply, "But I really do believe in God! I pray to Him, and I know so much about Him. I was even baptized." There are three things here I'd like to unpack. First, let's start with the claim that you believe in God. Read James 2:19: "You say you have faith, for you believe that there is one God. Good for you! *Even the demons believe this,* and they tremble

---

4. A. W. Tozer, *The Crucified Life* (Grand Rapids, MI: Baker Publishing Group, 2011).

in terror" (emphasis added). Why would the demons tremble if they believe in Jesus? The Jesus I know is my compassionate friend! It's because they are no friend of His. They know that He has authority over them, and so they despise Him. Yet they *believe* in Him. In scripture we see that demons possessed a man, and they spoke to Jesus because they knew who He was and feared Him. Yes, they believed. So we see that even the demons believed in Jesus, spoke to Jesus, knew much about Jesus, and even obeyed Him when Christ spoke. Luke 10:17 says that the disciples joyfully reported to Him that "even the demons obey us when we use your name!" Yes, they believed in Jesus. But is that enough?

Second, knowing and quoting scripture must prove we are saved, right? We've memorized verses from Bible school and Sunday school. We participated in Bible drills in our youth. Mark 1:24 (ESV) says, "What have you to do with us, Jesus of Nazareth? Have you come to destroy us? *I know who you are—the Holy One of God*" (emphasis added). Yes, they know who He is. They themselves quote scripture. So what is that missing link? Jesus is certainly not who they want to identify with. They bow a knee to no one except Satan. Yet they believe in God. It's clear that the belief they own is the belief of existence and being factually true but not a belief of love, repentance, and surrender. Psalm 119:11 (NIV) tells us the right reason for our knowing or memorizing scripture: "I have hidden Your Word in my heart, that I might not sin against You." If this is your motive for knowing scripture, you are surely blessed. "Every word of God is pure; He is a shield to those who put their trust in Him" (Prov. 30:5 NKJV).

Third and last, but of great importance, is our need to understand the significance of baptism. We've all witnessed comical scenes in the baptistery. I watched in great amusement as a pastor was baptizing a young boy. It was evident to everyone in the congregation that the top of the boy's head never made it into the water. The pastor hesitated for just a second before he knew he *must* dip him again! Everyone enjoyed the laugh. There have been times when extra-large people being immersed caused the water to rise above its walls and splash onto unsuspecting choir members. And occasionally someone's feet will slip, and we see both of them fly up as their head went under. Sometimes there are giggles even at important events. And baptism is definitely one of those most important events. But what is baptism? *Are you hanging your salvation on the fact that you were baptized?* If so, that is as sure as using peanut butter to glue on a chair leg. It will collapse. Listen to the scripture pastors share as they baptize someone: "Therefore we are buried with him by baptism into death: that like as Christ was raised up from the dead by the glory of the Father, even so we also should *walk in newness* of life" (Rom. 6:4 KJV, emphasis added).

To be clear, baptism is in obedience to the Lord's command. It is the beginning of a new life of obedience to Christ. But baptism is merely a representation or a picture of what has already occurred in your life. Baptism is a public testimony to all in attendance that you understood you were a sinner in need of God's forgiveness. It says that you repented of your sin and have made a choice to follow Jesus for the rest of your life. It's making a declaration to the world that you love Jesus Christ for the sacrifice He made for you on the cross. It signifies that you have joined a new camp and will seek to further God's kingdom here on earth by telling others of His amazing grace. It is all those wonderful things. But the one thing it is not is salvation.

> **But our salvation is in the *finished work of Jesus* on the cross and not anything else.**

There is a denomination that insists scripture says we are to be baptized in order to have forgiveness and be saved. But our salvation is in the *finished work of Jesus* on the cross and not anything else. To add to salvation by deeming we must be baptized expresses your belief that there is just *one more work* that must be done in order for us to be saved. We must do something. But that is a wrong belief. We see in Luke 23:43 that baptism is not a prerequisite for salvation as Christ lovingly told the one thief, "I assure you, today you will be with me in paradise." This man died before he could be baptized. Was he just an exception to the rule? Here is the rule: We need to do nothing more than repent and turn by faith to Jesus to be saved. But God wants us to make our private decision very public through baptism to glorify God and show others that we are now different.

Jesus sees our hearts. He knows everything that lives there. And there is nothing that can be hidden from Him. Hebrews 4:13 says, "Nothing in all creation is hidden from God. Everything is naked and exposed before His eyes, and He is the One to whom we are accountable." Many people put on masks (by the way, the word *hypocrite* refers to this very thing) and can persuade others to see them as someone or something they are not. Sadly, they are so good at this game that they have inadvertently fooled themselves into believing they have a genuine faith. John 2:23-24 says, "Because of the miraculous signs Jesus did in Jerusalem at the Passover celebration, many began to *trust* [believe] in Him. But Jesus didn't entrust Himself to them, because He knew all about people. No one needed to tell Him about human nature, for *He knew what was in each person's heart*" (emphasis added). Here we see that even though there was a "type" of belief, Jesus did not accept them. Why? He recognized that their belief was in His works and miracles. They had no desire to invest or live their lives for Jesus. They just wanted what He was giving away. These people were calling Him Lord, yet they were hypocrites. In Luke 6:46 Jesus says, "So why do you keep calling me 'Lord, Lord' when you don't do what I say?" They wanted what He could do for them. Sadly that describes so many today.

Is it really scriptural to "accept" Jesus into our hearts? We've all heard that term used in sermon messages about accepting Jesus as our Lord and Savior. I believe for the most part that when this is said, it's with pure intentions. But still, we need to be mindful of these words from A. W. Tozer that point out a deformed view some in the church have that must be righted:

> The doctrine of justification by faith—a biblical truth, and a blessed relief from sterile legalism and

unavailing self-effort—has in our time fallen into evil company and been interpreted by many in such a manner as to actually bar men from the knowledge of God. The whole transaction of religious conversion has been made *mechanical and spiritless.* Faith may now be exercised without a jar to moral life and without embarrassment to the Adamic ego. Christ may be *received* without creating any special love for Him in the soul of the receiver. The man is "saved," but he is not hungry nor thirsty after God. In fact, he is specifically taught to be satisfied and is encouraged to be content with little. How tragic that we in this dark day have had our seeking done for us by our teachers. Everything is made to center upon the initial act of "accepting" Christ (a term, incidentally, which is not found in the Bible), and we are not expected thereafter to crave any further revelation of God to our souls. We have been snared in the coils of a spurious logic that insists that *if we have found Him, we need no more seek Him.*[5]

How sad to turn an opportunity of having a personal relationship with God into something that removes any involvement of our heart—only our head. And head knowledge is not a spiritually transforming knowledge. Please recognize that tradition or habit or desire to not want to appear needy is as harmful as throwing water on a hot ember. In essence this is equal to quenching the Spirit, which is a sin. When the Spirit beckons, we cannot afford to ignore His voice and then continue in our religious habits. God's Holy Spirit is often represented in scripture as a flame and represents the presence and power of God. To hold fast to denominational traditions that are external in nature only or to continue a habit formed generations ago within your family is to shun what is most important—the

---

5. A. W. Tozer, *The Pursuit of God* (Chicago, IL: Moody Publishers, 1995), emphasis added.

conviction of the Holy Spirit in your life. Even trying to convey to others that you've got it all together, appearing to be something *more than you are* indicates a soul that has not yet bowed a knee in humble submission to God. Our external religious rituals and ideas turn into idols that we place above Jehovah God. I've heard it mentioned that it's the red carpet of the Methodist church or the stained glass windows of the Baptist church or even the grandeur of the Catholic church that holds prominence in the hearts of men. So we must ask ourselves, *Do we hunger and thirst for the righteousness of God?* Scripture tells us we are blessed if we do. To hunger for righteousness is to yearn for God's rule in our lives. It is to have a thirst for God's Word and for godliness.

> To hunger for righteousness is to yearn for God's rule in our lives. It is to have a thirst for God's Word and for godliness.

This personal story is one that depicts what a genuine faith or belief in God looks like, albeit wobbly at times. My faith was genuine, but that did not exclude me from the doubts and fears the enemy threw at me. Genuine belief in the Lord God will catapult you into going where you never thought you'd go and doing what you never thought was possible. Genuine belief in God is when we place ourselves, our lives, fully in the capable hands of our Father. This is only possible when we really trust our Father and believe His words. Trust is so precious that to ever have a trust broken with someone results in having to rebuild that trust. And its growth is excruciatingly slow. But when we fully put our trust in God, that's another story! He is faithful to keep His promises to His children, and we will never regret the day we surrendered all to Him.

Forced Faith

> *Therefore I will boast all the more gladly about my weaknesses, so that Christ's power may rest on me. That is why, for Christ's sake, I delight in weaknesses, insults,*

I BELIEVE IN GOD, SO I'M SAVED, RIGHT?

in hardships, in persecutions, in difficulties. For when I am weak, then I am strong. (2 Cor. 12:9-10 NIV)

We can all say we have faith until the time comes to use it! My husband had always sung in the choir as well as sang in quartets and performed solos. Music was a huge part of his life. I was the adoring wife, always seated safely in the pews enjoying it all. But there was a time in my life, a particular moment in time, when I committed to the Lord to "do the hard things." It's the easy things that we love to do, and we go away with a sense of accomplishment for the Lord. But it's those "hard" things that we cringe at the thought of actually doing. So much so, we usually end up letting go of the opportunity to really step out in faith.

It's almost annoying how quickly the Lord heard my statement of commitment to Him! However, what followed was something I never in a million years thought I would do—because I was afraid.

My husband and I were almost in the car after church one morning. Another minute and I would have escaped! But instead, in the Lord's timing, the music director came up to me and asked if I would be the narrator for this year's Christmas music with our choir. As I had practiced in my mind doing, I said "Yes" without hesitation. It wasn't until we were leaving the parking lot that I almost fainted! Did I mention that it was only July? That meant I had six full months to practice . . . and to think about my lines. The problem was this (and mind you, the Lord already knew what my problem was): He was going to allow me to experience firsthand, up close and personal, that His grace was sufficient for me.

I had developed anxiety in high school, but at that time, no one ever talked about it. I didn't even know it had a name. All I knew was that I had it, and it could be debilitating whenever it reared its ugly head. As an adult, I had learned somewhat to manage it. I had even taken medication for it but took myself off, not wanting to become dependent. I would not put myself in situations that would cause my anxiety to expose itself. It's easy to manipulate things when you're an adult because we can always excuse ourselves and leave whatever it is that is making us anxious. But not this time! I said "Yes" without giving myself a chance to be a coward.

Fast forward to about the last of October. By that time I'd attended rehearsals with the choir. I had discovered that my position to narrate would be just to the left of the choir, at my own music stand. I was to be hidden in the darkness until the time for some lines of narration. Then a spotlight from who knows where would come on, blinding me. In fact, I was being *showcased!* That's something a person with fear of speaking in public does not want! It was necessary for me to buy a tiny clip-on book light to clip onto my copy of music and narration in order for me to even see my words. The spotlight made it so I could see no one in the audience nor my words. Hence, the tiny book light.

So it was now about six weeks before the choir's performance when severe panic attacks set in. I didn't let my husband know. There was nothing he could do to help, and it would stress him out as well. He'd just say, "Tell them you can't do it." But I was determined to do it no matter what! I was going to trust the Lord even if doing so was terrifying. Many times I would get up in the middle of the night to go to another room where I couldn't be heard, and I'd pull my knees into me and hold them tightly and cry and rock and pray and pray and rock and cry. I begged the Lord to take away this horrible anxiety! My heart raced and thumped like it never had. I'd take fast, long walks around the pasture during the evening to try to calm me down. As I walked, I prayed, and I cried. My heart raced violently. And all the while Satan beamed with delight as he anticipated that my trust in Jesus was drying up. Apparently, he had no idea who he was dealing with.

Finally, the time came. Not only was there a performance on one night, but for the first time it was decided that we'd have two performance nights! This was so that more people from the community might be able to come. This was turning into the biggest nightmare of my whole life.

I was a very good actress both nights. No one would have guessed what was going on inside me. The prayers were continually running through my mind. But when it was time for me to narrate, God saw me through. I spoke calmly and distinctly, and someone actually asked me later if I had been trained as a professional speaker! Can you imagine? The first night was a success. I was elated at how the Lord had provided a calm voice, and my timing was perfect where I had to come in during the music. I had been able to see my words pretty well thanks to the little book light.

But there was still one more night to go. My nerves were not diminished one bit. If anything, I was more afraid because I now knew exactly what it was going to be like. But, just like the night before, the Lord gave me the voice, the courage, and the ability to not fall down with trembling legs. However. . . .

This is the spot in the story that still makes my heart race, but in a good way. At the end of the second performance, at the end of my last line to speak, immediately after my closing word, my book light went out! Without the light, I could see nothing on my page, but it didn't matter because God had seen me through it all. It appears that He held back those nasty demons that Satan loves to turn loose on God's children until they could do no harm.

I believe I'm still praising God even today for the grace He showed me and the great lesson in using my faith, no matter how small, to His glory and for my faith to grow. Do I still doubt what I can do? Yes, because in my own strength I can do nothing. But "when I am weak, then I am strong." *Thank You, Lord Jesus, for Your amazing ways of growing Your children, especially when we are under pressure. You are faithful to keep Your promises!*

EXAMINE YOURSELF

Are you believing rightly? Or have you misunderstood what it means to believe?

Which definition of "believe" do you live?

Are you clinging to tradition and habit to be your "righteousness"?

Are you exercising your faith and belief in God's power and grace?

Do you believe He is able to see you through?

When was the last time you really stepped out in faith, allowing God to be the one in control?

Pray, asking God to open your spiritual eyes with the leading of the Holy Spirit to a sincere belief in God—one that puts you at the front lines of His will.

Chapter 2

PRAYER

May my prayer be set before you like incense; may the uplifting of my hands be like the evening sacrifice.
—Ps. 141:2 (NIV)

Many people pray to God especially when there is trouble in their lives. I've found that even blatant unbelievers will pray to *something* when they are scared enough. Pastor Adrian Rogers said, "There are too many spiritual forgers signing Jesus' name to their prayer checks."[6] You may wonder, however, if the fact that you pray proves that you're a Christian. After all, you close your eyes and say His name, asking for something. You even say, "In Jesus' name." The answer is not necessarily. This only proves that you know what prayer is and that you are in need. God absolutely hears all prayers ever uttered to Him. Nothing gets past Him. But, please understand this: God is not *obligated* to answer the prayers of the lost. And God is not *accountable* to anyone. Even if you wrongly think you are saved, your words are still floating in air.

---

6. Adrian Rogers, *Adrian Rogers Legacy Bible,* Acts 19:11-17 (Memphis, TN: Love Worth Finding Ministries, NKJV) 1,245.

I BELIEVE IN GOD, SO I'M SAVED, RIGHT?

Pastor J. Vernon McGee said, "God's ears are closed to the prayer of the wicked. The wicked have put off doing the most important of all things on earth. He has refused to come to Christ and, in humility, acknowledge his sorry state and great need for salvation."[7] First Peter 3:12 (NIV) says, "For the eyes of the Lord are on the *righteous* and His ears are attentive to *their* prayer, but the face of the Lord is against those who do evil" (emphasis added). Here is where you may say, "But I don't do evil!" Scripture tells us that those who reject Jesus as Lord of their lives are enemies with God. That is evil. Keep in mind, however, God is God and can do anything He desires to do. Nothing prevents God from answering a prayer, whether you are His child or not, *if it is His will.*

Did you know that there are different postures a person may assume as they pray? The Bible tells us of people who prayed standing with arms raised. Many bowed their faces to the ground on their knees while others were prostrate on the ground in complete humility and submission. Does our posture when we pray affect how our prayers are heard? No, but the posture of our heart will choose the posture in which we choose to pray, for sure. A humbled spirit cannot stand before our great God except in utter adoration and lowliness. Certainly God is only concerned about the posture of our *hearts* as we pray. Are we praying in a spirit of repentance and surrender? God knows. But why would God want His creation to pray? What is God's motivation for giving us the great privilege of prayer? First and foremost, we must remember that *all* things are for God's glory. We sometimes think we are the center of the universe when it's actually God. We somehow think that everything God does is to make us look good by giving us that great job or to make us feel better by

> **Does our posture when we pray affect how our prayers are heard? No, but the posture of our heart will choose the posture in which we choose to pray, for sure.**

---

7. Pastor J. Vernon McGee, *Valdosta Daily Times*, "Prayers of the Wicked" (September 18, 2021) from valdostadailytimes.com.

resolving a family issue. But step back a moment. Realize that God is bigger than the universe. His divine purposes are far above our understanding. And we think it's all about us!

God loves us so much He desires fellowship with His children. In fact, scripture tells us that we were made for His pleasure (Rev. 4:11). He knows that we need His guidance, His protection, and His peace because He is our Father. Listen to what God Himself wanted us to know about our struggles in life as we read Ephesians 6:12 (NIV): "For our struggle is not against flesh and blood, but against the rulers, against the authorities, against the powers of this dark world and against the spiritual forces of evil in the heavenly realms." God knows our great need for Him because without Him we are powerless. We all need lessons in humility, and prayer reminds us that we are not in control. *But God.*

What is God's motivation for answering our prayers? Is it so we will like Him more? Of course not. However, answered prayers can be a convincing witness to those who doubt God. Even unanswered prayer is healthy for our faith as it teaches patience in God's timing and trusting that God knows what's best. There will be many times we don't understand why God has not answered our desperate prayer or why He answered seemingly so late. We may even question the way He answered. But the fact is, we may never know the answers to many of our questions until we are face to face with God in heaven. And then, it won't even matter! We will one day understand everything and will be so grateful that God in His infinite wisdom chose to answer our prayer the way He did.

But also understand this: to the Christian, God is our Father. We are in His family. We belong to Him, so He is *attentive* to His children. Romans 8:15-17 tells us, "So you have not received a spirit that makes you fearful slaves. Instead, you received God's Spirit when He adopted you as his own children. Now we call Him Abba, Father. For His spirit joins with our spirit to affirm that we are God's children. And since we are His children, we are His heirs." He is perfect in every way and sovereign over all things. So if God chooses to answer the prayer of an unbeliever, He can. There is, however, one prayer of an unbeliever that God will always answer eagerly and passionately and immediately. That would be the prayer of genuine repentance.

Ask yourself why you pray. What is your motivation behind it? To whom are you really addressing? Do you understand that if we saw God for who He is in all His glory, we would not be able to stand? Exodus 33:20 (NIV) says, "But God said, 'you cannot see My face, for no one may see Me and live.'" This verse has been often misinterpreted, but when understood correctly we see that God is so glorious that no man can see Him and casually go on with life as normal. This verse is referring to the fact that to really see God is *life altering*. From an article entitled, "No Man Can See My Face and Live: Seeing God's Face,"[8] we are told this means "no one can see God's face and continue to be revived and strengthened by *natural* means. No one can look directly at the Creator of Genesis 1 and simply call it a nice experience."

You may have read the scripture reference in Isaiah 6:1 (NIV), which says, "In the year that King Uzziah died, I saw the Lord high and exalted, seated on a throne; and the train of his robe filled the temple." That gives the visual image that God is so huge in stature that there were flowing yards and yards, if not miles, of a royal robe train filling the temple. But further research reveals an even greater description of the majesty and power and greatness of God. The great monarchs of Egypt and Assyria, earthly kings, wore very elaborate robes. Whenever a king defeated another camp, he would cut off the defeated king's train, and it would be sewn onto the end of his own train. This was to make a loud statement to all who saw his gloriously lengthy train! It was obvious that he'd been victorious in countless battles. As we think about God's gloriously long train filling the temple, we understand this depicts One who is almighty and victorious over all. There is no battle He cannot win; in fact, there is none

---

8. Fellowship of Israel Related Ministries (FIRM), "No Man Can See My Face and Live; Seeing God's Face," by Doug Hershey, "What seeing God's face does to us" (January 28, 2016) from firmisrael.org.

He has not won! After all, He defeated death! This picture of a majestic robe's train represents God's unbelievable glory. First Chronicles 29:11 says, "Yours, O Lord, is the greatness, the power, the glory, the victory and the majesty! For all that is in the heavens and in the earth is Yours. Yours is the kingdom, Lord, and you are exalted as head above all."

We all are familiar with the story of the burning bush in the desert found in Exodus 3:1-14. Moses was shepherding his flocks when he saw a bush ablaze, but it was not consumed. So he decided to go closer and take a better look at this strange thing. He wondered why the bush was not being burned up to ashes. God's eyes were on Moses, and as he got closer to the bush, God called his name. Moses replied, "Here I am." Then God said, "Do not come any closer. Take off your sandals, for the place where you are standing is holy ground." Then He said, "I am the God of your father, the God of Abraham, the God of Isaac and the God of Jacob." At this, Moses hid his face, because he was afraid to look at God.

> Many are guilty of downsizing deity to fit their small mental frame of Him.

This amazing God who yearns for our prayers, who loves us with an everlasting love, who gave up the very best He had, His Son, so we might have life; this same God who spoke just the word and everything on earth and in the heavens was created, who knows the name of every star; this same God who parted a sea only to close it again on the entire Egyptian army; this same God who raised Lazarus from the dead and gave Sarah a child at age 90, who commanded demons to depart, who shut the mouths of ravenous lions for Daniel; this same God who hung on a cross and still gained the heart of one crucified beside him—this is the same God some come so casually to, asking Him for things as if He were a slot machine or a genie in a bottle. Can we not see how utterly fearful we should be to even think about approaching such a divine Creator as our God? Many have invented a God of their own understanding. Many are guilty of downsizing deity to fit their small mental frame of Him. Yet and still, as we have already discovered, He wants His children, those who are born again into His family, to call Him Abba, Father, because He loves us, is merciful to us, and is abounding in grace. What a grave disservice we do to ourselves when we limit God's power, His authority, and His Sovereignty by our small ideas. What arrogance humanity displays as some attempt to create their own personal god, keeping him on a short leash, allowing him just enough power to take care of their selfish desires.

How big is our God? "My thoughts are nothing like your thoughts," says the Lord. "And my ways are far beyond anything you could imagine. For just as the heavens are higher than the earth, so my ways are higher than your ways and my thoughts higher than your thoughts" (Isa. 55:8-9). The Bible tells us in Luke 20:43 that God will humble Christ's enemies, making them a footstool for His feet. As the song written by Hillsong states,

> *Death could not hold You.*
> *The veil tore before You.*
> *You silence the boast of sin and grave.*
> *The heavens are roaring the praise of Your glory*
> *For You are raised to life again!*
> *You have no rival!*
> *You have no equal!*
> *Now and forever God You reign!*
> *Yours is the Kingdom!*
> *Yours is the glory!*
> *Yours is the Name above all names!* [9]

When I was a young believer, I loved God, but my prayers were immature spiritually because I was still growing in my faith and in my understanding of His Word. Mostly I prayed to have urgent needs met, like a new refrigerator, or that my child would get well, or that my husband would get that great job. None of these things are wrong because God loves us so much He wants us to come to Him with everything. But as I grew older and

---

9. Hillsong, "What a Beautiful Name," written by Ben Fielding/Brooke Ligertwood (Australia: Hillsong Publishing).

my faith in God matured, I found myself praying just because I loved Jesus! I had no agenda. I just wanted to praise Him for Who He is and thank Him for giving me His great salvation. God owes us nothing. Yet He gave us His all.

Here is an amazing personal story of how God answered the prayer of a desperate child of His. Again, I'm reminded that God owes us nothing, but because He loves us so much, He delights in hearing the prayers of all His children. What we may consider a miracle, God simply sees it as His grace.

Against Impossible Odds

If you abide in me, and My words abide in you, ask whatever you wish, and it will be done for you. (John 15:7 ESV)

God's Word tells us that "with God all things are possible" (Matt. 19:26 NIV). I believe that with all my heart. But when I saw it play out in my own life, I realized that maybe I hadn't fully believed it until I saw it. *Forgive me, Lord. But thank You that, in spite of faith the size of a mustard seed, You still work wonders on behalf of Your children, whom You love.*

Daddy was a man of simple means. He was happy with a plate of fried squirrel and all his girls around the supper table. He was happy with the baying of his beagles on the scent of a rabbit. Simple pleasures to him equaled a good life. And don't we all know that he was right? To pick one of his own ripe tomatoes off the vine, to go to the hardware store and shoot the breeze with his buddies, to put on that suit and tie and tuck his Bible under his arm—these were the simply beautiful things of my dad's life. There may have been a thing or two he didn't quite get *tied down* like they should have been. But he did the best he could, and his family loved him with all our hearts.

Dad died on December 2, 2015, at the age of eighty-seven. I didn't shed one tear at his funeral because, honestly, I wasn't sad. I was relieved for him. I was relieved for my sister who cared for him. I was relieved that Daddy had finally found home. Mom was heartbroken, of course, but she didn't camp there. Meaning she loved this man with all her heart but knew also that he was now in the company of Jesus as well as so many of his saved friends who had passed before him. She knew without a doubt she'd also be seeing him again. When you know these things—and really believe them because of what the Bible says—death is a jubilant time because we know that Christ defeated death!

    But now, all the legal mumbo-jumbo was to begin. Two of my sisters who lived near each other in Arkansas took care of everything. What an undertaking and responsibility! As time passed, we soon realized that the insurance company that Dad had worked for, which incidentally had changed hands many times, was not going to honor my father's life insurance policy. My sister, the caretaker, worked tirelessly gathering the necessary paperwork, trying to connect the dots where dots were missing. She wrote letters, made phone calls, sent copies of this and that, and jumped through all the hoops trying to resolve this issue. It was exhausting. But sadly, nothing came of her efforts except that it pushed us to plan B.

    My sister willingly passed over to me all that she'd gathered, all the important and necessary papers she'd compiled over many months. I took on the challenge of finding an answer. So having no money to pay for a real attorney, but knowing an attorney was going to be necessary, I decided to use a local law firm that does not collect a fee unless they win the case for you. That was as real as I could afford. That's where I met a wonderful attorney who worked in a nearby town. I visited his office once to drop off the paperwork, talked to him several times by phone, and then returned once again to his office to pick up the same paperwork. He had done what he could but said there were too many "holes" left unattended in Dad's insurance papers.

    When I returned home with my hopes dashed and a bundle of pages that had been earmarked over and over with yellow sticky notes identifying the problem on each page, I wanted to cry. I knew Dad had done the right thing in obtaining life insurance for his family. He had known before he died that

PRAYER

he had a $19,000 insurance policy. The insurance company had begrudgingly squeezed out a check for less than $85 payable to Mama. I don't know what that was for, but it was my understanding that she didn't cash it. It wasn't necessarily pride keeping her from doing that. It was a broken spirit.

So I prayed. And I prayed. And I prayed. And the Lord set my heart ablaze with an idea! What did I have to lose? I ran up to the office where I began to bang out a letter on the computer. It wasn't argumentative. It wasn't accusing or even angry. I wrote a letter to the insurance company president and pleaded for him to view this with his heart and not his brain. I introduced him to the man Daddy was. I let him peek into the life of my family with four young daughters. I begged him to respond in a humanitarian way and not look at us as a small annoying problem to be brushed away like a fly. We were real, living, breathing people who had an injustice done to us, and we had no way to prove it. I told them I had prayed that the Lord would open their eyes and their hearts to do what was right. My husband and I prayed over the sealed letter containing the words of a daughter who knew her Jesus was going to intervene, and then I mailed it.

Time passed. And it passed slowly. But burning within me was an absolute assurance that the Lord was going to honor my letter. I can only say it was the Holy Spirit speaking to my heart, telling me to not lose hope—that He is always the answer. Then the phone rang. . . .

My husband picked it up, and it showed it was an unknown number. Instead of letting the caller leave a message, my husband actually answered the call and extended his hand to me. I said, "Who is it?" He said, "I don't know." I said, "Hang up. I never answer unknown numbers." Remember, the caller could hear our conversation! So, through a somewhat comical skirmish, the call was cut off. A few minutes later the phone rang again from the same number. This time, I answered. It was Dad's insurance company! A woman told me they had received my letter and were heartbroken over the turn of events. She told me they had fired the person responsible for turning away our requests. I believe my sister had been in touch with that person. This lady on the phone was apologetic and said that she'd never read a letter like that before in her life and had to get to the bottom of this tragedy. She then added that a check for $19,000 was on its way to Mom!

That was it! In just a few minutes, God had fully answered my prayer. There are no words to describe the victory dance and shouting that happened then. I called my sister immediately and told her the Good News. The *unbelievable* news! This was the same giant insurance company that an investigative TV program had just done a piece on uncovering corruption and deceit. This was the same company that, for some inexplicable reason, a stellar attorney couldn't work with. But this is the company that the Lord God Almighty chose to prove Himself to be mightier than any CEO. Scripture tells us that God can "turn" the hearts of men in authority for His purposes. And that's what He did.

> **When prayer is your lifestyle, you walk in the power of the Holy Spirit.**

Praying to God is life's ultimate privilege. And when prayer is your lifestyle, you walk in the power of the Holy Spirit. Imagine the God we have just read about bending His ear to hear our small voices as we cry in fear, wring our hands in worry, curse Him in anger, and reach out to Him for strength to carry on another day. Have you ever said, *Amen*, opening your eyes with the feeling that God has now left the room? Do we think He's resumed doing what He was doing before we started our prayer? That's a thought I've had before. But then I remembered that *amen* doesn't mean "goodbye!" *Amen* simply means "so be it." It's a way of ending our prayer time. Yet how exhilarating to realize that although we may have said our *amen*, He's gone nowhere. He's still right there with us. He never leaves us! He has gone before us and is behind us and lives within us. Our *amen* is simply the beginning of a whole day spent with God in our presence. So remarkable! He made us for Himself, and He delights in us.

So before we nonchalantly lean back in our comfortable bed, barely parting our lips to pray to the Almighty before we nod off, maybe we need to be sure that we know just who it is we're speaking to. To someone who doesn't love the name of Jesus or follow His ways or revere His name in public, they may want to take a step back and reevaluate their motive for praying to a God they may not really be acquainted with. Is God your lucky charm, or is He your Lord and Master?

EXAMINE YOURSELF

Do you pray because you see God as your Abba, Father?

Do you see your weakness and need God's strength?

Are you confident He will answer you because you are His child?

Do you love God, or are you in a tough spot, trying to gain favors from someone you don't even know?

Are you humbled to think the Creator of all, God, revels in hearing His child call out to Him?

Chapter 3

TESTIMONY

But this will be your opportunity to tell them about Me.
—Luke 21:13

You've probably heard people give their personal testimony of when they first came to saving faith in Jesus Christ. We've all heard astonishing testimonies not unlike the apostle Paul on the Damascus Road. Then we've heard others that seem low-keyed and not dramatic. (Although, salvation is a gloriously dramatic miracle whether our description of it is or not.) Yet I've heard a "testimony" or two that didn't quite make the mark. Meaning, something was missing. It was just a facade. If your testimony (personal story of how you were saved) doesn't include the phrase "I was a sinner bound for hell" or the word *repentance*, then you have no testimony. Scripture tells us that until we are saved, we are all enemies of God. And until we see our sin, we will never see our need for a Savior! Something life-changing must occur to make us children of God. What is it? *It's called repentance.*

I BELIEVE IN GOD, SO I'M SAVED, RIGHT?

The definition of our Christian testimony simply means to share with others about our relationship with God and how we came to faith in Him. Psalm 107:2 says, "Has the Lord redeemed you? Then speak out! Tell others He has redeemed you from your enemies." Of course, if you are not a true believer, then you don't have a personal testimony. If you have told someone you are a Christian, but you've never been saved, you're going to feel like a hot spotlight is on you should anyone ask. True, not everyone is comfortable speaking to others in a group or maybe even one on one about when they surrendered their life to Jesus. That's understandable. I used to suffer greatly from anxiety. Speaking in public in general caused me to lose sleep and stress horribly. But one day I ran across these words, and they have been invaluable to me ever since, allowing me to take advantage of times I could share my faith: "Speak the truth even if your voice shakes." God will take our lame, weak, trembling words and empower them to accomplish what He wants them to. That gives me the confidence I need to open my mouth and share to the glory of God! But there are other ways we may share our testimony.

> God will take our lame, weak, trembling words and empower them to accomplish what He wants them to.

God absolutely expects us to *voice* our love for Him because it's easy to look like just another "good person" to others. Without our neighbors understanding that it is *because of Jesus* that we do what we do, it's easy to blend in with the morally good. Keep in mind there are more ways to connumicate than just verbally. Who we are is exhibited through our daily lives. We actually are a living proclamation of what we hold to be true. If you enjoy writing, you may find that expressing yourself more accurately is easier if you send someone a note. How special for someone you know and love who may not know Jesus as Lord and Savior to receive a personal note from you. Because writing notes, letters, and cards is slowly falling by the wayside, it makes it even more special that someone would take the time to write, especially about something as personal as our relationship with Jesus. I have no doubt they will feel blessed as they read it. Whenever I write something of spiritual value to someone, I always pray before I mail it that God will bless the words that I chose and give those words power to achieve what only His Spirit can do.

I recently came across an article I wrote some time back regarding witnessing by writing. I hope writers will find it encouraging.

> *I call myself and others who love to write about Jesus Evangelistic writers. All my life I have loved to write and am able to express myself more clearly through the tips of my fingers than through my lips. I know God definitely has given us a mouth to proclaim the Good News, and I've been faithful to that command, although while speaking I may stumble through my words, forget a scripture verse because of nerves, or in other words, in my estimation, do a poor job. But I also know God empowers my words for His glory and will use my weakest and puniest words to accomplish His will. However, I still love to write about Jesus, and I love to explain the scriptures through the written word. I have to admit there have been many times I felt foolish and stupid for writing a letter to a loved one or a friend because of their response to it. The devil has me beating myself up with me asking myself, Why did I choose to write such a long letter? Why did I walk off that cliff like I did by giving them a letter? Everything I write drips with kindness and is offered in sincere love because I let the Word of God do the offending. God's Word definitely offends those who don't believe—it's called conviction. So as I have thought about the hundreds of letters I have written over the course of many years, wondering if this approach was wrong, the Lord reminded me of something this morning that revives my spirit! The New Testament is twenty-seven books.*

I BELIEVE IN GOD, SO I'M SAVED, RIGHT?

And of those twenty-seven books, twenty-one of them are letters! Yes! God used letters to reach people during New Testament times. Of course I will still use my mouth to talk about Jesus whenever I get a chance one on one with someone God has put in front of me. But I also will more confidently continue to write my letters to those who need to hear the truth. God gifts His children, and I know He has gifted me with the love of writing. So to all of you Evangelistic writers—don't stop! Be encouraged that you are not the first nor will you be the last person to influence another by your God-empowered words.

Another way to share your testimony with others is by the way you live your life. We are being observed whether we realize it or not. *Righteousness should be the pattern of a redeemed life.* How many times have we, ourselves, taken note of something a neighbor was doing or what kind of friends they have over? We can tell by literature in our friends' homes, whether they pray at meal times, and by their language. Our lives really do have an impact on others. So as they see you week after week, month after month, and year after year, loading up your car with the family and heading out for church, you're making a silent impression on someone.

> **As they see you week after week, month after month, and year after year, loading up your car with the family and heading out for church, you're making a silent impression on someone.**

If you know that a friend or neighbor is ill, going by their house to take them a dish is so nice, but dare to go one step further. What few people do is *pray* for them. Before leaving, spend two minutes praying for God's blessing on that person and that they feel His peace and presence in their life. This will be a treasured moment for them, I guarantee. Because no matter how calloused or stubborn someone may be, to have someone care enough to pray for them is unexpected and nourishing to their soul. What a great testimony for God.

TESTIMONY

I want to share my personal testimony with you as I feel it will resonate with many who find themselves "believing" in God but have not genuinely repented and followed Christ.

Prone to Wander

We all like sheep have gone astray, each of us has turned to our own way; and the Lord has laid on Him the iniquity of us all. (Isa. 53:6 NIV)

I was born in Memphis, Tennessee, and lived most of my childhood on Holmes St. near the University of Memphis and the famous Mid-South Fair. We moved there when I was five years old. At the age of thirteen I was attending Sunday school at Southern Avenue Baptist Church. I don't remember attending with much regularity, but I do remember one Sunday being in class, not even aware of what the lesson was about. Just waiting for the bell to ring. I looked around at the other girls, and I didn't know them. I felt pretty alone. Finally, the dismissal bell rang, and everyone began to leave the classroom. I must have been the last one to leave because my Sunday school teacher walked over to me and asked if I wanted to be a Christian. In her defense, that is a pretty good question to ask. But surely she knew I had not been coming much. Surely she saw I really didn't know what was going on. I was just there.

So what would any agreeable and shy child do? I said, "Yes." Being a Christian didn't sound like a bad thing. It's just that I didn't really know what being a Christian was except for *believing in Jesus*. I could see she was happy and asked that I follow her to the pastor's study. I dutifully followed this unknown woman through halls I knew nothing about and ended up at the pastor's study.

I remember getting on my knees at his leather sofa and saying what the pastor told me to say. This was the "Sinner's Prayer," but there are, of course, no magical words in it that will save a person. We have to have a heart that is *wanting* the Lord to become our Master for it to have any meaning at all. I walked out of that office an unchanged thirteen year old, but in their eyes I was born again.

I don't remember having any more meetings with my mom or dad or the pastor or the teacher. All I remember next is being in the baptismal pool, watching my other sisters being baptized with me. That's it. But I received a letter from the church congratulating me on coming to Christ and being obedient through baptism. It was official. It had a date and signatures and the whole shebang. I must be saved!

Year after year went by with no noticeable change in who I supposedly had become. I think I'd heard something about becoming a "new creation in Christ"? But I certainly hadn't seen it in myself. Around the age of eighteen or nineteen, I'd been living a life of complete degradation. I was a mess. I never had a thought of God. Never had regret. Just did as I pleased even if my conscience sometimes nagged me. I brushed those feelings to the side immediately to continue down my chosen path of sin. But I was so unhappy. I believe I chose that lifestyle for acceptance and so-called friendship. That's just the way any lost teen or young adult would think. I wanted to be like the others, not stand out. But in trying to blend in, I almost lost my whole life.

It has occurred to me all these years later the many times God spared my life. I can remember some episodes like it was yesterday, and I can see now that the hand of God was on me. Why did I make it through while some do not? I don't know, except to say that God loved me and was seeking me. And God had a purposeful life planned for me, and He desperately wanted me to find that plan. If my spiritual eyes had been opened, I have no doubt I would have seen scores of angels surrounding me in that out-of-control car, keeping me awake at the wheel, in that bar inebriated, keeping my date from wrecking, keeping me from falling victim to the predators I encountered, and keeping me from dying from what I labeled "fun." But God protected me because He had so much more for me. God was seeking me relentlessly. He wanted me to *know Him*. He pursued me! John 6:44 says, "No one can come to Me unless the Father who sent

Me draws him." I can hardly believe that the God who sits on His throne in heaven pursued *me*.

Eventually I found myself faithfully serving the Lord and loving His Word. I taught children's classes and women's classes as well as led Bible studies. But God put some doubts into my head about my salvation—not about whether I was saved or not but *when* I was saved. Certainly not at age thirteen. I had only walked through the rituals that time with no real heart change. But here I was at sixty-five years old, working for the Lord with a heart that was thrilled to do so. I had worked in VBS, and I went on a couple of mission trips that I'll cherish always. I knew I was saved because I was the opposite of who I once was and had a heart sold out to God. So when was I saved?

One day I began to think of my life on a timeline. I was reminded that when we are saved, a *new life* begins. I began to examine my life to see just when it was I saw a transformation. We are to turn 180 degrees from following our own sinful desires to following the desires of Christ. I wanted to find out when it was I saw an actual *difference* in how I lived and thought. Jeremiah 29:13 (NIV) says, "You will seek Me and find Me when you seek Me with all your heart." I was seeking, for sure! After much prayer and reminiscing, I came to a conclusion that put my heart at ease. After I was married at age twenty-two, my husband and I began attending a country church together. I realize now that God was bringing all this to my mind! Years back, we had attended several old-time revivals there at that church, and I began to recall a time during one of those revivals when I felt God's strong conviction on my life. I realized that standing in a pew during a wonderful, Holy-Spirit-filled service, I repented of my sin, and it was then God saved me.

But the only thing was this: *I thought I was already saved, remember?* So I thought I was just "rededicating" my life to Christ. Turns out, God saw my heart; for the first time it was filled with genuine repentance, and I was saved then at about age twenty-three. It was at that time I saw on my personal timeline the transformation take place in my life. But here's what I want you to see: If you'd asked me when I was fifteen or eighteen or twenty-one if I was a Christian, I would have said yes—*simply because I "believed" in God.* I believed He existed, but I had never surrendered my life to His Lordship. By God's amazing grace, I had escaped hell. So how do you live your life after realizing something that monumental? You live it wholly surrendered to Jesus. There is no other way.

EXAMINE YOURSELF

Do you have a testimony that admits your lost condition, asks for God's forgiveness, and thanks God for His amazing grace?

Do you yearn for others to hear your testimony so they might be saved?

Are you a "changed" person?

Are you interested in the testimony of others?

Do you feel like you are being personally challenged when you're asked to share, or do you count it a privilege?

What is your testimony? Tell it often, even if it's just to yourself. This will remind you of who you belong to and will glorify God.

Chapter 4

REPENTANCE

Repent, then, and turn to God so that your sins may be wiped out, that times of refreshing may come from the Lord.
—*Acts 3:19 (NIV)*

First John 1:9 (NIV) says, "If we confess our sins, He is faithful and just and will forgive us our sins and purify us from all unrighteousness." Let me share some insights on the definition of repentance:

> The word repentance in the Bible literally means, "The act of changing one's mind." True biblical repentance goes beyond remorse, regret or feeling bad about one's sin. It involves more than merely turning away from sin. In the Old Testament, repentance or wholehearted *turning to God* is a recurring theme in the message of the prophets. Repentance was demonstrated through such rituals such as fasting, wearing sackcloth, sitting in ashes, wailing, and liturgical laments that expressed strong

sorrow for sin. But these rituals were supposed to be accompanied by *authentic* repentance that involved a *commitment to a renewed relationship with God, a walk of obedience to His Word and right living.* Often, however, these rituals merely represented remorse and a desire to *escape* the *consequence* of sin.[10]

True biblical repentance is characterized by four elements:

1. True repentance involves a sense of awareness of one's own guilt, sinfulness, and helplessness.

   Against You and You alone have I sinned; I have done what is evil in your sight. You will be proved right in what you say and your judgment against me is just. For I was born a sinner—yes, from the moment my mother conceived me. But You desire honesty from the womb, teaching me wisdom even there. Purify me from my sins, and I will be clean, wash me and I will be whiter than snow. Oh, give me back my joy again; You have broken me—now let me rejoice. Don't keep looking at my sins, remove the stain of my guilt. Create in me a clean heart, O God. Renew a loyal spirit within me. (Ps. 51:4-10)

2. True repentance apprehends or takes hold of God's *mercy* in Jesus Christ.

   Have mercy on me, O God, because of your unfailing love. Because of your great compassion, blot out the stain of my sins. (Ps. 51:1)

3. True repentance means a change of attitude and action regarding sin. Hatred of sin turns the repentant person away from his or her sin to God.

---

10. Gotquestions.org, "What Does the Bible Say about Repentance?" Emphasis added.

> Each of your commandments is right. That is why I hate every false way. (Ps. 119:128)

4. True repentance results in a radical and *persistent* pursuit of *holy living*, walking with God in obedience to His commands.

> But God's truth stands firm like a foundation stone with this inscription—The Lord knows those who are His, and all who belong to the Lord must turn away from evil. (2 Tim. 2:19)

Jesus called all sinners to repentance.

> *I have not come to call the righteous, but sinners to repentance." (Luke 5:32 NIV)*

> *But unless you repent, you too will all perish. (Luke 13:3 NIV)*

What we believe about sin will determine what we believe about salvation. (Dr. Robert Jeffress)[11]

> **We still have a sin nature lurking inside us. It is not removed when God saves us. That is why there will always be conflict between our flesh (what we want to do) and God's Spirit living in us.**

Here's another very simplistic life story: As much as the sinner must repent before there can be true salvation, even God's children—those of us who are already saved—must repent *daily* for sins that we either knowingly or unknowingly commit in order to keep a right relationship or fellowship with God. We still have a sin nature lurking inside us. It is not removed when God saves us. That is why there will always be conflict between our flesh (what we want to do) and God's Spirit living in us. This illustration applies to the lost as well as the saved.

---

11. Sermon by Pastor Robert Jeffress entitled, "What Every Christian Should Know about Sin," from the Pathway to Victory program sponsored by rcg.org online.

I BELIEVE IN GOD, SO I'M SAVED, RIGHT?

Let's say your children were roughhousing in the living room and accidentally broke a vase, knocking it to the floor with a football. They know instantly they've messed up. So now they are at the crossroads of, *Do I hide what I did?* or *Do I confess and say I'm sorry?* Let's say they decided on the first option. They grab the glue, and the vase is back to looking just like new. They are thrilled with the results and see no reason to say anything to you. However, later in the evening, as you lay your keys on the side table, you notice a line running through your vase. You also know what has occurred. You decide to wait to see if there is any remorse/conviction followed by confession and repentance. You wait, and you wait. You long for a confession. There is none. As a parent, your heart is broken because they are trying to hide their sin from you. You ache for your child to come to you, confessing, so that you can have the joy of showing them *grace*, telling them it's OK and that you forgive them. But they don't come. The first brick of a wall dividing parent from child has just been laid. Their relationship remains the same—they are still a family. But their fellowship has just suffered a blow.

True repentance comes humbly and in *agreement* with God that we're sinners. Don't think sin is a big deal? To repeat what my pastor has said, we have in our own minds *minimized* what sin is. We think surely God won't count that against us because it was such a small thing. But what we are not taking into account is *Who it is* we've sinned against. Sin, to be clear, is *rebellion against God*—outright war. And as the created ones, we do not have the right to determine how severe our punishment should be. My pastor gave this illustration: If a young boy was at school and punched another boy in the nose, what do you think would happen to him? He'd be held in detention. But then what if when he saw his teacher he punched her in the nose as well? What do you think would happen to him? He'd be suspended. Or what if one day he sees a policeman and punches him in the nose? What would happen to him? He'd probably be arrested. But then years go by, and one day the President of the United States walks toward him, and this young man then lunges toward the President and punches him in the nose. What would his consequences be? He'd probably be shot dead. As you see, the sin was the same in each occurrence. But the severity of the punishment is determined by the one in authority who the sin was against. We cannot challenge God's authority! And if it is against God, the Bible says that the wages of sin is death as God Himself has determined. That is why there must be true repentance before there can be forgiveness. Sin is an egregious act against an all-powerful and holy God!

"Repent or you will all likewise perish" (Luke 13:3 KJV). True repentance is a hardy acknowledgment that we have failed God. We must be willing to renounce our sin, unwilling to continue our claim on it. We cannot come in repentance to God with our sin still tucked away in our back pocket. Dwight L. Moody said, "Man is born with his back toward God. When he truly repents, he turns right around and faces God. Repentance is a change of mind. Repentance is the tear in the eye of faith. There are men today who are in darkness and bondage because they are not willing to turn from their sins and confess them; and I do not know how a man can hope to be forgiven if he is not willing to confess his sin."[12] True repentance comes from a heart that realizes we've done wrong, we've sinned, and we are in need of forgiveness. True repentance comes from a broken spirit looking for God's grace. Want grace? Want forgiveness? Scripture says in 1 John 1:9 (KJV), "If we confess our sins, He is faithful and just to forgive us our sins and to cleanse us from all unrighteousness." Hebrews 8:12 (NIV) says, "For I will forgive their wickedness and will remember their sins no more." Psalm 103:12 (NIV) tells us, "As far as the east is from the west, so far has He removed our transgression from us." Daniel 9:9 (NIV) says, "The Lord our God is merciful and forgiving even though we have rebelled against Him." Acts 3:19 (NIV) says, "Repent, then, and turn to God, so that your sins may be wiped out, that times of refreshing may come from the Lord."

---

12. Dwight L. Moody, "Repentance is a Change of Mind," sermon from family-times.net (2023).

And finally, look at how God *delights* in our repentance: "I tell you that in the same way there will be more rejoicing in heaven over one sinner who repents than over ninety-nine righteous persons who do not need to repent" (Luke 15:7 NIV).

True repentance can only come from a heart that is committed to surrendering fully to the Lordship of Jesus Christ. Oh, please, dear friend, read that again! And without repentance, there can be no salvation.

EXAMINE YOURSELF

Does this describe your life?

Was there a specific time in your life when you made the decision to repent and be saved?

Is it your heart's desire to be holy as Christ is holy?

To assume your sin is minimal is an outrageous misconception. And to just assume you will go to heaven without repenting is a death sentence. Will today be the day you stop lying to yourself and see how your pride and love of self is keeping you from having a personal relationship with God?

Chapter 5

WORKS AND GOOD FRUIT

A good tree produces good fruit, and a bad tree produces bad fruit.
—Matt. 7:17

What about my good works? *you may ask.* Don't they count for anything? I am a good person. Doesn't that prove that I'm saved? There are many in the church today who are busy doing "God's work." They are on three committees, they sing in the choir, they participate in bake sales for the church, they serve as greeters at the doors on Sunday mornings. They even tithe. But why? What is their motivation for their busyness? Many are counting on their good outweighing the bad when they stand before God. They have a works-based idea of salvation. And by believing this way, they are declaring that Christ's death on the cross was *not enough* to save anyone; that we must add to what He did on the cross by doing good works. Scripture tells us in Ephesians 2:10 (NKJV), "We are God's workmanship, created in Christ Jesus *for good works,* which God prepared beforehand that we should walk in them" (emphasis added). So we see that *works* is indeed an integral part of the Christian life. But how exactly do works come into play? Ephesians

2:8-9 (NIV) tells us, "For it is by grace you have been saved, through faith—and this is not of yourselves, it is the *gift* of God—not by works, so that no one can boast" (emphasis added).

Christianity teaches that salvation is a free gift of God through faith in Christ, and no amount of work or effort is necessary or even possible to get to heaven. Salvation comes by our faith in God and His grace. Even our faith is given to us. The Bible emphasizes that faith is a gift because God deserves all of the glory for our salvation; we cannot do enough good works to earn our way to heaven. If salvation was based on our works, we would all be destined for hell because *God Himself* is our perfect standard. It is unfathomable for a sinful, imperfect person to trust in his good works to gain heaven. How can good works like mowing an elderly person's lawn, not cursing, or having perfect attendance at church put someone anywhere near the mark of perfection that God is? Unbelievers have chosen to let the *good* they've done through the years be their passage to heaven. And if that is the standard of righteousness they choose to use, God will allow it. But it will never be enough because, against the backdrop of God's holiness and perfection, our works are worthless. God's holiness is our standard, and we can in no way measure up. That's why He provided a way because God knew that without His Son dying for us, we'd all be without hope.

> If salvation was based on our works, we would all be destined for hell because *God Himself* is our perfect standard. It is unfathomable for a sinful, imperfect person to trust in his good works to gain heaven.

Sometimes we hear people say about another, "He says he's a Christian, but there is simply no fruit in his life." What does that mean? What is Christian fruit? What is it that they are not seeing in that life? Galatians 5:22-23 (NIV) says, "But the fruit of the spirit is love, joy, peace, patience, kindness, goodness, faithfulness, gentleness, and self-control." These are the things that come out of a person who has been filled with the Holy Spirit when they've been saved. So the *fruit of the Spirit* is referring to the fruit or results that come from having the Spirit of God living in us. And this fruit will *always* be fully evident.

Is it visible in you? As much as it is obvious that a ball game is being played in a stadium, that is how evident our works or fruit will be in our lives. But if you go to a stadium and it's empty and quiet, no one has to tell you that there's no game being played. Matthew 5:16 tells us, "In the same way, let your good works shine out for all to see, so that everyone will praise your heavenly Father." It will be glaringly obvious to believers that something is missing because God's Spirit gives us spiritual discernment. Scripture says in James 2:18, "Now someone may argue, 'Some people have faith; others have good deeds.' But I say, 'How can you show me your faith if you don't have good deeds? I will show you my faith *by* my good deeds.'" I know people who say they are Christians yet they are seldom at church if ever; they do not associate with the believers at a church or elsewhere; they help in no way in advancing God's kingdom by serving others, visiting the sick, praying with the brokenhearted, donating money, or teaching someone about Jesus. They resume their lifestyle of selfish behavior. Possibly including ungodliness and immorality or just plain apathy, claiming it's their life and they will live it the way they want. They don't understand that a *saved* life is a *changed* life.

What must be true for a tree to produce fruit? It must be a living tree. A dead tree cannot produce fruit. So also is the life that doesn't possess God's gift of His Holy Spirit. Without Christ to make us spiritually alive, people, lost without the Holy Spirit in their lives, are dead men and cannot produce godly fruit. When someone claims to be a Christian, we should be able to look at their life and see evidence of godly fruit. What does godly fruit look like?

First, let's notice what the works of a sinful nature look like—what an unchanged, unrepentant heart displays. For sure, it is not godly. Because of our sinful nature, we bear things such as idolatry, jealousy, slander, gossip, arrogance, dissensions, fits of anger, sexual immorality, and lust for earthly pleasures. But because we are Christians, we *want* to bear fruit that is in keeping with our relationship with God. We seek to do things outwardly that demonstrate that we have been made new in Christ. *It's a supernatural longing to serve Jesus just to glorify Him.* Truly, this can only be possible because we are now brand new creations, born again in the likeness of Christ. We are not who we once were. A person who is not saved will not and cannot have this kind of desire. So what is the key to bearing godly fruit? To bear fruit in the Christian life requires abiding in Jesus. It is God who does the work in us; our fruit bearing is simply a result of what *He* does. Jesus commanded, as John 15:4-5 (ESV) says, "Abide in me, and I in you. As the branch cannot bear fruit by itself, unless it abides in the vine, neither can you, unless you abide in Me. I am the vine; you are the branches. Whoever abides in me and I in him, he it is that bears much fruit, for apart from Me *you can do nothing"* (emphasis added).

> To bear fruit in the Christian life requires abiding in Jesus.

Let me share what the supernatural power of God can do in a life. I'm talking about *my* life. God tells us that apart from Him, we can do nothing. I can personally say that without God's Holy Spirit living in me, I would choose to do *nothing* for His kingdom. I would be happy to wake up and go about my day, working or running errands and being the one who writes her own agendas. But through His salvation, the Holy Spirit transforms our ordinary, unregenerate hearts into something that is truly miraculous. It then becomes impossible to conceal your good works because obeying Jesus becomes our greatest desire.

I was given the opportunity to go on a mission trip to Haiti with my church. I'd seen others through the years go on these trips and listened to their reports with interest but had no desire to go myself. One year, however, God's Spirit gripped my heart to the point that I questioned nothing, disregarding all that was necessary for the trip. It just didn't matter to me. I was set on going, and nothing was going to stop me. As I now look back, I am amazed at how resolute I was. I signed up. I had no concern about cost. I'm not sure I even asked my husband's blessing! I was to be the oldest person going at the age of sixty-four.

WORKS AND GOOD FRUIT

    I had a fear of flying, boats, traffic, bodies of water, buses, heights, bugs, motorcycles, and agendas that were not written in stone. I experienced every one of these things on my five-day trip with absolutely no trepidation. I actually had to take five flights to get there and back. I rode in an open boat powered by an outboard motor across a stormy ocean for two hours with ten-foot crests where I became so nauseated I had to be helped to the bus after making land. I rode behind unknown Haitian men on the back of motorcycles up the side of a mountain to get to an orphanage. I rode a hot, rusty bus with windows that didn't work, among many other things. We drove up mountainsides with steep drops on the other side. Traffic was horrific as Haitians made their own traffic lanes whenever they chose, driving at reckless speeds. And I only encountered two roaches at the compound where we stayed that were almost large enough to trip over. I still am proud of the bravery I exhibited as I beat them to death with a broom and then went to sleep in my netted bed in peace. All I felt on the entire trip was the perfect peace and presence of God. I experienced no fear, and I attribute that completely to the grace of God. All I wanted to do was to, each day, share the love of Jesus with the Haitian men, women, and children that we ministered to.

    Of all the things that I went through with my fellow travelers, what I remember most were two things: the beauty of the Haitian sky at dawn and at sunset, and the sweet face of a woman my age, blind in one eye, who became my friend even though we didn't speak the same language. She understood the name "Jesus" and smiled when we'd say it together. And I know I'll be spending eternity with her. How was I able to do all this? What caused me to forget all my fears and step into a world I knew nothing about? And a quite dangerous world at that, one that needed to know Jesus. It was God in me. And when you follow God, hang on! Living your life for Christ's sake is the most amazing and rewarding life you could ever live. There was no hiding that fruit. *Thank You, Jesus, for using me, such a weak vessel, to share Your name with the lost to grow Your kingdom.*

So we need to ask ourselves at this point, *Do I desire to do good works to glorify God? Or am I looking for compliments and recognition? Are my "works" based on how others will see me or accept me? Is my motive for doing good to make me feel important or give me purpose?* Matthew 6:1 warns, "Watch out! Don't do your good deeds publicly, to be admired by others, for you will lose the reward from your Father in heaven." We need the supernatural draw of God's Holy Spirit within us—proof that we are saved—before we can ever have the sincere desire to die to ourselves and our wills so we may glorify God.

Seeing the Fruit

> *But Jesus called them to him saying, "Let the children come to Me, and do not hinder them, for to such belongs the kingdom of God." (Luke 18:16 ESV)*

Sometimes God smacks me right in the face with evidence He's still working. That's always a fun time because it's a surprise. And I love a surprise!

I have taught Vacation Bible School (VBS) since my daughter was a baby. I've led classes, worked in crafts, as well as been the director over several age groups. I've always enjoyed the creative side of teaching because kids seem to pay attention better if they're doing something fun or making something or listening to exciting lessons. But I've never, ever lost sight of the fact that the bottom line is always to teach the children about Jesus and what He did for us. I wanted them to understand how much God loves us—that He allowed His only Son to come to earth and be ridiculed and crucified just for us. I'd explain that sin is what drags us to hell but that by trusting in Jesus as the Master of your whole life, we can live in heaven. The gospel is simple, so teaching children about it was also simple.

Here is the definition of Murphy's Law: "A supposed law of nature to the effect that anything that can go wrong will go wrong."[13]

---

13. "Murphy's Law," from Google's English Dictionary by Oxford Languages.

That pretty much describes VBS, except Christians know that many times it's those pesky demons turned loose to try to wreak havoc on the best laid plans of teachers. The devil most assuredly does not want children learning about Jesus or coming to saving faith. It just so happened that one year, during the set-up days where we were getting our rooms in order and working on decorations and lesson plans, my department of children was given a whole house to meet in that was on the church property. It was basically four rundown rooms. It had no working bathroom, the windows were painted shut, and to just add insult to injury, the air conditioning unit was not working. At least this was before it was filled with hot, wiggly kids. It's hard to imagine that even God could work a miracle under those conditions! How well can the Holy Spirit really work when the Kool-Aid is warm, and the sweat drops are rolling? Actually, that's when we see Him working best.

Things like that were always expected. Would the copier be working? Would the air conditioner hang on? Or just any number of random things. But in the end, everything always worked out. God can still be heard in the middle of chaos. Children were fed God's Word, friendships were forged between the children as well as between the workers. Fun was had by all. This had been a particularly difficult VBS for my department because of the aforementioned problems, but I do remember explaining to the kids almost every morning how simple the gospel is and that it is usually the adults who want to make a simple thing difficult. Children have such a pure and trusting way of seeing things, whereas adults always want to clutter up things. We wrapped up another week of VBS and went home exhausted but full of joy.

The following Sunday, I was still recovering from fatigue and an overused brain. My husband and I were sitting in the pew, and someone was going to be baptized. I saw in the bulletin it was a child I'd had in my VBS class. It's not unusual at all for many kids to be saved during Bible school, but I hadn't heard a word about this. As the youth pastor was talking to him in the baptistery, the pastor said, "I've talked to Nick and asked him who it was that was responsible for leading him to the Lord. He told me it was Miss Sheila Rogers." I almost fell over! I didn't know he'd asked Jesus to save him! He must have gone home and talked to his parents, who in turn talked to the pastor. I somehow got left out of the conversation, but that's OK, because for as long as I live, I'll always hear in my head that *Miss Sheila Rogers led a young boy to the Lord!* Hallelujah! What a privilege! Now, we all know that it was only through the power of God's Holy Spirit speaking to this young boy's heart that he was saved. But just think about it: God used me to help save a soul! Me!

EXAMINE YOURSELF

Where do your greatest desires lie?

Based on what you've just learned about works and fruit, are you producing godly fruit that points others to Christ, or are you just busy because it makes you feel useful?

Do you feel your time is yours to spend as you wish, or do you have a heart's desire to serve God wherever He wants you?

Is advancing God's kingdom here on earth a priority to you?

Chapter 6

OBEDIENCE

For this is the love of God, that we keep His commandments. And His commandments are not burdensome.
—*1 John 5:3 (NASB)*

To a genuinely saved person, Jesus is the center of their universe! Just as the planets rotate around the sun, Christ is to be central to everything we do. He is our purpose for living and the One who sustains us. Our greatest desire is to *obey* Christ Jesus and serve Him. No one has to bribe us, and there are no pangs of guilt that force us to have this supernatural desire. Our genuine "want to" is to obey.

If obedience to Christ, which is the same thing as the call to follow Christ, is missing from your life, there's a problem. I once heard a pastor say simply that obedience to the Lord is *proof* of salvation. Obedience does not earn us salvation. It simply is a reflection of the existing desire in your heart to honor God. You can believe everything the Bible says and have it memorized from cover to cover, but without obedience to it, you're no different from the demons

> Obedience to the Lord is *proof* of salvation. Obedience does not earn us salvation. It simply is a reflection of the existing desire in your heart to honor God.

who believe. Why is that? Because if there is no surrendered life to the lordship of Christ (as assuredly the demons do not), there will be no conviction to obey God. Imagine a marriage where your spouse is *almost* surrendered to being faithful to you. Would that be good enough? Of course not! You want someone who is one hundred percent surrendered to being faithful to you. *Almost* says, *I will not obey our covenant of marriage*. Why would we think Christ could be satisfied with anything less? Obedience parallels with a surrendered life. And genuine salvation is a picture of both.

Do we really understand that God owes us nothing? God did not have to send Jesus to die on the cross. God is under no obligation to forgive anyone for anything. God didn't *need* men inspired by the Holy Spirit to record anything for us to have in the twenty-first century. But God is gracious and loving and kind beyond our comprehension. God, who made the world and the people and all that there is, including you, lovingly chose to let you know *who He is* and how to live by giving us His scripture. There is no way to know God without knowing His Word. Luke 6:46-47 says,

> *So why do you keep calling me 'Lord, Lord!' when you don't do what I say? I will show you what it's like when someone comes to me, listens to my teaching, and then follows it. It is like a person building a house who digs deep and lays the foundation on solid rock. When the floodwaters rise and break against that house, it stands firm because it is well built. But anyone who hears and doesn't obey is like a person who builds a house right on the ground, without a foundation. When the floods sweep down against that house, it will collapse into a heap of ruins.*

OBEDIENCE

There are consequences for not reading God's Word. Do you want to know truth or be deceived? John 14:15 (NIV) tells us, "If you love me, keep my commands." That's about as concise as you can get.

Before we read other verses that relate to our obedience to Christ, let's take a moment to look at our lives to see just who it is we've put on the throne of our hearts—because whoever that is, that is who we will obey. Do we casually wear the badge of "Christian" but then live our lives according to our will? Are we good with *most* of what God says but firmly disagree with a few things, choosing to honor our wishes and beliefs over God's desires? If so, we are the ones who sit on the throne of our hearts that rightfully belong to God. We've placed our desires and our decisions above God. *We have become our own idols.*

If obedience to the Word of God is essential in proving genuine salvation, then we must know what God's word says so we may obey. Pretty simple. But where do we begin? We open the Bible, ask God to give us understanding, and read. Colossians 3:1-3 says, "Since you have been raised to new life in Christ, set your sights on the realities of heaven, where Christ sits at the place of honor at God's right hand. Think about the things of heaven, not the things of earth. For you died to this life, and your real life is hidden with Christ in God." That simply says, if you want to live obediently in Christ, you must seek to know His Word and then strive to obey it daily. Can we do that perfectly? Of course not, because, remember, that old nature still lurks inside us all. But instead of living like the old nature rules us, we are to live like the Holy Spirit rules us. We are to set our minds on learning what is godly and not what is worldly. This is a very intentional thing. A deliberate choice we must act on.

What are some things we might find within the pages of the Bible that will show us how to do that? God tells us to forgive others as He has forgiven us. God tells us to give to others cheerfully, helping the widows and the orphans. He instructs us to obey our leaders and submit to their authority.

Christ tells us that we are to be imitators of God. He tells us to listen to the wise instruction of our parents and to honor them. We are not to murder or be unfaithful to our spouses. We are to repent of our sin daily and praise God at all times and in all things. God tells us to love everyone—even the unlovable. God tells us that it is our duty to share the gospel with all. God tells us that every battle belongs to Him and that we are to trust Him in all things, giving Him all the glory. God says to pray without ceasing. He tells us to not put anything above Him in our hearts. God tells us to not neglect meeting together with other Christians. He says to not be conformed to the world but be transformed by the renewing of our minds. God says to hide His Word in our hearts (memorize). We are not to associate with the occult in any way. God tells us to think of others as more important than ourselves. He hates a prideful heart and warns that pride comes before a fall. God wants us to serve Him in ways that glorify Him. God says to flee sexual immorality. God says we are to love Him with all our heart and with all our soul and with all our mind. We are not to kill innocent life, as in abortion, and warns us that marriage is between one man and one woman. There is no end to the instruction God gives us in His Word that we are to obey. First Samuel 15:22 says, "But Samuel replied, 'What is more pleasing to the Lord: your burnt offerings and sacrifices or your obedience to his voice? Listen! Obedience is better than sacrifice, and submission is better than offering the fat of rams.'"

There is no way to know what pleases God or how to live according to His will apart from reading the scriptures. You may argue that you can't clearly understand the Bible, so allow me to provide an illustration I once heard from a teacher. She said that her parents were married just days before the young husband was shipped out to join forces fighting in World War II. Their love was so strong and pure for each other as newlyweds, and they would cling to every word that was shared between the two of them by letter. However, because of restrictions in what could and could not be written for concern of disclosing information that was classified, whenever the young wife received a letter from her husband, there were many parts of the pages that had been cut out, censoring what could be potentially harmful. Since he wrote on both the front and back of each page, there were large gaps in his sentences that she couldn't make out—pages and pages of a love letter cut to pieces. But still the young bride was overjoyed because although she couldn't understand everything he had written, she could read enough to know that he loved her. That's the same way we can view our trying to understand scripture. Our understanding will increase over time, and there is much that we may never understand. But we can still understand enough to know God loves us.

There are so many versions and translations that, with just a little help from a Christian store clerk, pastor, or Christian friend, you will be able to find one that speaks to you clearly. It's worth the effort to read different versions of say John 3:16. You might want to also research what the differences are between versions and translations. For instance, the NLT (New Living Translation) is a paraphrase of scripture, making it a bit easier for many to read at first. But none of us are able to understand all of the Bible. For one thing, we must have the Holy Spirit within us to understand spiritual things. A person must be saved. Also, God tells us that some things are a "mystery" even to believers. But we still read and pray, asking God to open our eyes to understanding—and He will! The more faithful we are to study the scriptures, the more God will reveal to us. In the same way, *the more faithful we are to obey God's Word, the more He'll reveal to us*. Why would God reveal even more understanding of scripture if we do not obey what He's already shown us?

> **The more faithful we are to obey God's Word, the more He'll reveal to us.**

To say you "believe" in God but have no time for His scripture in your life and no desire to obey what it says means there is no salvation. A changed heart, one that loves God, will love His Word. The more you read it, the more you will understand it and love it. Jesus Christ Himself is called The Word. An unrepentant heart that has not experienced God's supernatural saving grace has *no desire* to hear the words of a god he does not love.

Let's read what God Himself has to say about obedience. Reading and studying the Word of God is intertwined with obedience because, without reading the Bible, we will not know what God wants us to obey. We must first have a knowledge of what is on the pages of Genesis to Revelation.

> *Anyone who belongs to God listens gladly to the words of God. But you don't listen because you don't belong to God. (John 8:47)*
>
> *I tell you the truth, anyone who obeys my teaching will never die. (John 8:51)*
>
> *If you love me, obey my commandments. (John 14:15)*
>
> *When you obey My commandments you remain in My love just as I obey My Father's commandments and remain in His love. (John 15:10)*
>
> *But He will pour out His anger and wrath on those who live for themselves, who refuse to obey the truth and instead live lives of wickedness. For merely listening to the law doesn't make us right with God. It is obeying the law that makes us right in His sight. (Rom. 2:8, 13—This is worth reading again.)*
>
> *And God will provide rest for you who are being persecuted and also for us when the Lord Jesus appears from heaven. He will come with His mighty angels, in flaming fire, bringing judgment on those who don't know God and on those who refuse to obey the Good News of our Lord Jesus. They will be punished with eternal destruction, forever separated from the Lord and from His glorious power. (2 Thess. 1:7-9)*

> *For the time has come for judgment, and it must begin with God's household. And if judgment begins with us, what terrible fate awaits those who have never obeyed God's Good News? (1 Peter 4:17)*

I think it is clear from just this sampling of verses that obedience to God's Word is expected of a person who has truly been saved. God does not require anyone to be obedient in order to *have* forgiveness of their sin. Remember, God's grace (His goodness) is what saves us. If we were required to obey to be forgiven, we would be inclined to brag about how obedient we had been when we were saved. In truth, God says you did nothing! But, as mentioned before, obedience is *evidence* of a heart devoted to God.

Is obedience easy? No, and no one ever said that it should be. But it is *essential*. Will we fail? Is it possible to always be obedient to the Lord? The following two scripture references will answer that question splendidly.

> *"What a wretched man I am! Who will rescue me from this body that is subject to death? Thanks be to God who delivers me through Jesus Christ our Lord. So then I myself in my mind am a slave to God's law, but in my sinful nature, a slave to the law of sin."* (Rom. 7:24-25 NIV)

These were the words of Paul who wrote thirteen or fourteen books of the twenty-seven New Testament books. He was a man wholly devoted to Christ yet hated his sin.

> *The Apostle Paul said, "I don't really understand myself, for I want to do what is right, but I don't do it. Instead, I do what I hate." (Rom. 7:15 NLT)*

When we are born again, we receive the gift of the Holy Spirit. But we do not lose our old sin nature. That explains why there is a constant battle raging within our souls. It is most often depicted in the comical way of having a devil sitting on one of your shoulders while an angel sits on the other. They are both whispering into your ears, telling you what you should do. And so the struggle begins. That's a close metaphor, but it still falls short. The struggle can be much less if *the Word* has been hidden in your heart, ready to be pulled up at a moment's notice.

Listen to this verse that many of us learned as little children: Psalm 119:11 says, "I have hidden your Word in my heart, that I might not sin against you." We will surely choose sin if left to our own devices because the "old self" still resides within us. But memorizing scripture is the most powerful weapon available in staying right with God. Why is that so? I have the perfect illustration about hearing the voice of authority. When my daughter was dating, we always trusted her to do the right thing and to never get into mischief. But having said that, we understood that our daughter was a normal teen who may or may not remember what the right thing is in the moment. So I always made it plain to her before she left the house to "remember what mama said." I was quite annoying, I am sure, as I repeated my instructions to her many times. I told her I wanted her to actually *hear my voice* inside her head when she was faced with temptation, knowing that hearing her mama's voice would be very disruptive to say the least! This is a weak illustration compared to the power found in knowing the scriptures, but whenever you have committed scripture to memory, God says He will provide a way of escape. That's why He tells us to hide His Word in our hearts (minds) so we may remember who we are in Christ and choose to do what is right in God's sight.

EXAMINE YOURSELF

Do you obey Jesus? Is He your standard?

Is faithful obedience to scripture your heart's desire?

Do you selfishly live each day according to your will and still believe you are saved?

Will you commit to setting aside time in your week to memorizing scripture?

Chapter 7

THE HOLY WORD OF GOD: THE BIBLE

For the Word of God is alive and active. Sharper than any double-edged sword, it penetrates even to dividing soul and spirit, joints and marrow; it judges the thoughts and attitudes of the heart.
—Heb. 4:12 (NIV)

Do you *love* God's Word? Can you sincerely say that it refreshes your spirit and that a day without reading the Bible is like a day without air? Is it your soft place to fall when your world is falling apart? Do you believe every word of the Bible? If you can't, then you can't believe any of it. It is not our prerogative to choose what is truth and what is not. God wants us to consume it cover to cover and to live our lives by it to His glory. Why is it essential that I *love* the Bible? What does it say about me if I don't?

Here is what a converted, born-again heart says: "For the *message of the cross* is foolishness to those who are perishing, but to us who are being saved it is the power of God" (1 Cor. 1:18 NIV, emphasis added). It has been a rule in our house for as long as I can remember that we set *nothing* on top of our Bibles. We don't use it as a coaster or a doorstop. We don't use it to sit a plant on. We don't use it as a footrest or have it lying about in an inappropriate place. This is God's Word! The very words on each page are God breathed and Holy Spirit inspired. Men, chosen by God, were used by God to write, using their own personalities, whatever the Holy Spirit led them to write. The Bible is without error or contradiction. It has been hated through the ages yet stands firm today. "All scripture is inspired by God and is useful to teach us what is true and to make us realize what is wrong in our lives. It corrects us when we are wrong and teaches us to do what is right" (2 Tim. 3:16-17).

Does the Bible hold value to you, or has it been sitting on that bookshelf collecting dust from ten years ago? Are its pages still crisp and new from disuse? I beg you to stop now and go find it. Knock the dust off, and open its pages. Breathe in deeply, and revel in the fragrance of God's love for you as you begin to read. I'm reminded of the statement that there is a scarlet thread that runs from Genesis to Revelation, meaning that the blood of Jesus Christ can be seen from the beginning of Genesis to the end of Revelation. All sixty-six books of the Bible are leading us to a personal relationship with God's Son. Now, you tell me if reading and knowing God's Word is important!

> **All sixty-six books of the Bible are leading us to a personal relationship with God's Son.**

When you hear someone quoting scripture, are you off-put? Do you feel like they are judging you by using scripture? When someone asks you what a verse means to you, do you go blank? Do you read scripture like you're reading "Aesop's Fables"? Do you see the Bible as a compilation of stories that only have moral meaning? Have you ever made comments on the Sunday sermon, seeing it only through a practical worldview? Take a moment to read this verse from Revelation 11:10: "All the people who belong to this world will gloat over them and give presents to each other to celebrate the death of the two prophets who had tormented them." To familiarize you with this story, the book of Revelation here is talking about End Times, after Christ has taken His church home at the Rapture and the world is now late into the Tribulation time. There will be two prophets chosen by God to do miracles and to preach the Good News. These two men will be so hated by the world that when God allows them to be killed, their bodies will be left in the street to decompose before the eyes of the world for the purpose of humiliating them and God. The world will be so thrilled by their deaths that they will celebrate by giving gifts to one another. But after three and a half days, God will breathe life into them, and they will stand up! Terror will strike the heart of every person on earth.

We are told in verse 10 that the *reason* the people hated the two prophets was because the *Word of God tormented the unbelievers.* Are you tormented by the Word of God? If so, please take a moment to assess what the real issue may be here. It's true that we all should grow in our faith, and as we do, our love for the scriptures will increase. But could it be more than just an immature faith making you want to run out of the room? Could it be that God's Word sounds like a foreign language to your heart, tormenting your soul?

There have been times I've shared a verse or two with friends or family, and it was received as judgment. That says something to me—they are burdened with the guilt of their sin and are not able to see God's Word as anything but condemning. Not only that, but they see the messenger as the one attacking them. How very sad! The Bible assures us that there is no condemnation for those who belong to Christ Jesus (Rom. 8:1). To a true follower of Christ, His Word is instruction for life.

> *How sweet are your words to my taste, sweeter than honey to my mouth. (Ps. 119:103 NIV)*

> *Your word is a lamp to my feet and a light to my path. (Ps. 119:105 NIV)*

I BELIEVE IN GOD, SO I'M SAVED, RIGHT?

You're my hiding place. I hope in your Word. (Ps. 119:114 ESV)

Great peace have those who love your law. Nothing can make them stumble. (Ps. 119:165 ASV)

How I delight in your commands! How I love them! I honor and love your commands. I meditate on your decrees. (Ps. 119:47-48)

God's Word is a love letter to every person! His promises are true. There is no truth except God's truth. But if we needed more reasons to love God's Word, hear this: "For I am not ashamed of the gospel, because it is the power of God that brings salvation to everyone who believes, first to the Jew, then to the Gentile" (Rom. 1:16 NIV). Why then would someone be bored with scripture? Why then would they think it's no more than God's condemnation on us? It is because they have not yet experienced the transforming power of God's salvation in their life.

Let's take a moment to discuss the things that you have come to believe to be true or have some merit. Many times people believe something to be true simply because they have never heard the real truth about it. For example, angels. What do you believe about angels? Have you heard that we've all been "assigned" a particular angel for life—a guardian angel? Do you talk about the power of angels more than the power of Christ? Do you see angels as cute little cherubs with rosy cheeks and chubby hands? Do you believe that when we die we become angels? Why do I ask these questions? Because every single one of these statements is false. They contradict what scripture tells us. Perhaps you've heard the statement, *If you don't stand for something, you'll fall for anything.* There is truth in those words. But it's more than just taking a stand for something. That *something* must be truth to begin with. When we are familiar with what is on the pages of the Bible, we will instantly see "red flags" whenever an untruth is spoken as truth. It's as if a glowing flare has just been launched. We first must *know* the truth to be able to discern what is not.

THE HOLY WORD OF GOD: THE BIBLE

My parents grew up in the country. Mom picked cotton and chickens! Dad plowed fields using a mule. Both their families were quite poor, and their education wasn't stellar. But my mom and dad were believers when they died. They taught my sisters and me so much about life. But, I have to add, I also heard what might be called old wives' tales from them that they shared as truth. Just because someone tells you something doesn't mean it's true! But if you never hear differently or you don't research its validity, you could go through life with some erroneous ideas. My father told me one of these things about mules that even today makes me smile. He said that mules attracted lightning, and that you weren't supposed to plow whenever a storm was approaching. He believed that because, I am sure, his own father taught him that. And I am guessing his father before him passed on that same information. Why is that wrong? Because mules themselves do not attract lightning! Perhaps the fact that they wear metal on them and pull metal plow blades, which are conductors of electricity, in an open field may have more to do with it than anything. But as you see, he even passed that down to me as truth.

Mom shared with me many years ago what she believed was the unpardonable sin. She said it was committing suicide. She said it was unpardonable because people didn't get a chance to repent of their last sins. At the time that made sense to me because I was young in my faith, and I'd never given much thought to it and had never heard a message about it. But one day her words came to my mind, and it wasn't until I really applied myself to thinking that I saw the error in what she told me. I realized that most people don't know when they're going to die, so no one essentially has *time* to repent before we pass on. But also, I knew that Christ died for my sins—past, present, and future—and that I had repented and was following Jesus as a believer. *I was already forgiven!* I was prompted to do my own study about the subject and found that the unpardonable sin is the sin of rejecting God's Holy Spirit when He convicts you of your need for a Savior.

My mom was wrong, but that's what she believed. She suffered from anxiety, and I attribute part of her ignorance of the Bible to the fact that getting out to church and Bible study was always a struggle for her. On those occasions when she was in church or Sunday school, she was not relaxed and was always distracted. I suspect that she was not able to stay focused when scripture was studied. However, I have no doubt she loved Jesus. We all have our Bibles at home where we can be alone with God and our thoughts and read. I'm sure she did this more times than I knew about. Everyone who calls themselves a Christian needs to make the effort to read what God so graciously has given us so that we won't be unnecessarily ignorant. Second Timothy 2:15 tells us, "Work hard so you can present yourself to God and receive His approval. Be a good worker, one who does not need to be ashamed and who correctly explains the word of truth."

In regard to this subject of the unpardonable sin, if today you are suffering under the guilt of your sin, understand this: God is waiting with arms open wide to receive you unto Himself. He is able to save completely all those who come to Him in repentance, seeking forgiveness of their sin. But rejection of His offer of salvation is indeed the unpardonable sin. Please don't wait until it is too late, for scripture tells us that the Spirit of God is like a wind that blows where it pleases. We can't see where it's going. How can we know if it will return to us? The time for repentance is when we first feel the tugging of God's Spirit on our heart. This is not something that can wait until tomorrow, for there may not be a tomorrow. Forgiveness is found *exclusively* in Jesus, and to reject the only pardon is to then choose hell over heaven. Please don't delay another second if you sense the urging of God's Spirit on your life to repent and follow Jesus. As the old hymn asks, "The Savior is waiting to enter your heart. Why don't you let Him come in?"[14]

When my father married my mom, they moved to the city where he sold insurance. He'd come home every day around noon to eat a bite and rest before heading back to work. One

---

14. Heritage Singers, "The Savior Is Waiting."

day I asked him if he'd mind us having a little Bible study before he had to go back to work, to which he was agreeable. I was a grown woman at this time and had never heard his story of how (or if) he'd been saved. I was so nervous, but it was important enough to me that I forged on. Since I was young, I didn't have any experience talking about the topic of salvation, so it was very awkward, and I didn't feel very prepared. I just did the best I could with God's help. As I talked about sin and hell, Dad looked off into the distance as he often did when he was thinking. He then said, "I don't think God sends anyone to hell." It was evident that he didn't know what the Bible says. He was going through life, now at the age of about forty-five, with the wrong idea about what happens to us after we die. Someone either told him that God loves us and is too loving to send any of us to hell, or, in his human reasoning, he deduced that if our goodness exceeded the bad, we would go to heaven. He wrongly believed that God's goodness would simply let us all into heaven, no questions asked. Along those lines, Pastor Adrian Rogers once said, "The worst form of badness is human goodness when human goodness becomes a substitute for the new birth."[15] It was sadly evident that my daddy, at least at that time, didn't understand Romans 3:10: "No one is righteous—not even one." Romans 3:23 tells us, "For everyone has sinned; we all fall short of God's glorious standard." Romans 6:23 teaches, "For the wages of sin is death, but the free gift of God is eternal life through Jesus Christ our Lord."

We've seen an inundation of men, women, and even children writing books about dying, going to heaven, and then returning to tell their story. Do you believe these to be true? Do you believe our loved ones who have passed away are watching as we live our lives? Do you think we are able to actually talk to our deceased family and friends? What are your views on subjects like reincarnation, horoscopes, coincidental happenings? Do you actually believe that because someone on their deathbed is

---

15. Adrian Rogers, *Adrian Rogers Legacy Bible*, Matthew 21:28-32 (Memphis, TN: Love Worth Finding Ministsries, Inc., 2009), 1,102.

a "fighter" that they had the power over God to determine the number of their days? What does the Bible teach us about those things? I urge you to do the research, and you will be astonished to find these ideas are without spiritual merit. Matthew 22:29 warns us about not knowing the scriptures. People had been asking Jesus a myriad of questions that were essentially not important, but they were weighing on their minds. Jesus answered them by saying, "Your mistake is that you don't know the scriptures, and you don't know the power of God." You'll find all the answers needed for life within the pages of God's Word.

> Many are embracing what their *human reasoning* is telling them is acceptable, but if society would but pick up God's Word and read, they would see "the human heart is the most deceitful of all things, and desperately wicked.

What kind of entertainment do you engage in either at home in private or out in a public forum that you believe is acceptable behavior for a Christian, rationalizing that it hurts no one? What about the language you use? Regarding our mode of dress, is there anything that you feel is inappropriate anymore, or has clothing that causes a man's eyes to roam and his mind to wander become our goal? These are but a random sampling of things our society has accepted as normal. Many are embracing what their *human reasoning* is telling them is acceptable, but if society would but pick up God's Word and read, they would see "the human heart is the most deceitful of all things, and desperately wicked. Who really knows how bad it is?" (Jer. 17:9). Proverbs 14:12 warns, "There is a path before each person that seems right, but it ends in death." Do we not see the eternal danger and consequences of living our lives apart from *knowing* what the Bible says? Sadly, even if it is read, most will not be able to comprehend it's meaning. Why? Again, we find the answer in scripture: "But people who are not spiritual [saved] can't receive these truths from God's Spirit. It all sounds foolish to them and they can't understand it, for only those who are spiritual can understand what the Spirit means" (1

Cor. 2:14). However, reading God's Word, even as an unbeliever, can plant godly truth into our minds that no doubt God's Holy Spirit can use to open eyes to salvation.

EXAMINE YOURSELF

Take a moment to think about how you view God's Word. Do you have a true spiritual understanding of scripture? Is it life to you, or is it mostly viewed as not pertinent, an annoyance, or just meaningless? Could it be that it terrifies you?

Do you see memorizing scripture as punishment and studying it a waste of time?

Do you understand that the Bible was supernaturally inspired by God's Holy Spirit?

Do you understand how making our own rules for life is a death sentence we have chosen for ourselves?

If your salvation is real, God's Word will be paramount in your walk of faith. God's Word is life.

Chapter 8

WORSHIP

Come, let us bow down in worship, let us kneel before the Lord our Maker.
—*Ps. 95:6 (NIV)*

Let's take a minute to think about places where we did *not* want to be in attendance. For me, that would be any sporting event. It could be a job that you despise. Maybe you obligingly went to someone's anniversary party whom you didn't care for. Or even a funeral of someone you were not close to, and the eulogy seemed unending. Perhaps you attended a lecture or study only to discover it was not to your liking—the subject nor the people. We've all been where we wished we could just slip out the back door, so why did we stay? Probably because it was the proper thing to do. It was being polite, or maybe it could have been to deceive others into thinking we were really enjoying ourselves. There are many other illustrations I could give, but the point is this: When we do not have a *genuine* desire to be somewhere, we are *miserable* until we can leave. We are not emotionally in agreement with what is going on.

Here again, we need to take time to examine our hearts. If you attend worship at a church of your choice, are you like a horse headed for the barn when the preacher says the final amen? Does your mind focus on the negative around you like the temperature in the sanctuary or someone's off-key singing? Do you cringe whenever it's time to take the offering, thinking, *Here we go again. They're always wanting my money*—? Do you try not to speak to anyone after the service because you think they're all weird, and you just want to get out of there? Scripture tells us plainly, "If someone says, 'I love God,' but hates a fellow believer, that person is a liar; for if we don't love people we can see, how can we love God, whom we cannot see" (1 John 4:20). Do you sit dry eyed through every message and hope no one goes forward during the invitation because that will only make church last longer? These are not good things to agree with. Why? What you've displayed is a heart that is not in tune with God's Spirit.

To be found guilty of some of these examples doesn't necessarily mean you are a lost person. It could simply mean there's something awry in your life that needs to be taken care of through prayer, repentance, and perhaps even godly counsel. But if this is the norm for you each time you go to "worship," you're what is called a true *hypocrite*. In times past, the word *hypocrite* was an acting term, meaning to put on a mask, to be something other than who you really were. Sometimes I will glance around an auditorium and see people, disengaged and distant, and I wonder if they're wearing this mask, just pretending to be engaged with the true worship of God. There is no joy on their faces or praise on their lips. They don't sing. They don't smile. They don't open their Bible. They may speak to others, but it has a feel of obligation rather than someone who's glad to be with fellow brothers and sisters in Christ. Many times, if a lost person has found his way into a worship service, and they see true believers lifting their hands in worship with tears and joyful singing, they may think it's all fake. They misinterpret our actions as habit or duty. The lifting of our hands is sometimes seen to the unbeliever as, *Look at me! I've got it all together!* I've actually heard this voiced, and I was shocked.

The longest sermon you will ever have to sit through is one that is not heard through the power of the Holy Spirit. It will feel laborious and tedious because you are wading through words that are meant to be digested spiritually, and you're not able to do so. Pastor Adrian Rogers said, "The devil would just as soon send you to hell from the pew as he would the gutter."[16] We can be in worship and be bound for hell. It's true that there is much that cannot be discerned by casual observation of people. So many of our friends and family have hurts and worries that we can't even begin to imagine, and we need to be sensitive to their needs and perhaps ask if we can pray with them. But there is something that will actually *distinguish* true worshipers from the false ones, and that is the presence of the Holy Spirit in our hearts.

In A. W. Tozer's book *The Purpose of Man*, he writes concerning "the path of heretical confusion."

> This is heretical worship in the correct meaning of the term. A heretic is not a man who denies all the truth; he is just a very fastidious man who picks out what he likes while rejecting what he does not like. Certain aspects of theology appeal to him, but others are rejected because they do not suit him at the time. I refer to these as inconvenient aspects of theology. A man once addressed a large group of Christian young people offering this advice: "Don't believe anything in the Bible that doesn't square with your own experience." This man had the infinite effrontery to tell young people searching for truth to take the Word of God and judge it by their little wicked hearts. How can you get any worse than that? It is heretical confusion at its best. Heresy means I take

---

16. Adrian Rogers, *Adrian Rogers Legacy Bible*, Matthew 23:13-15 (Memphis, TN: Love Worth Finding Ministries), 1,104.

what I like and I reject what I do not. The very word "heretic" means one who picks and chooses. But the Bible says, "And if any man shall take away from the words of the book of this prophecy, God shall take away his part out of the book of Life, and out of the holy city, and from the things that are written in this book." Rev. 22:19 KJV. The Lord rejects this path to worship because of its selective nature, picking what it likes and what does not inconvenience its lifestyle. If it does not like something, it explains it away and goes on as if it were a small matter or if it even did not exist.[17]

> The most unlikely people gathered under one roof will have a supernatural connection with one another because they each have a personal relationship with Christ.

"Fellowship is a mutual bond that Christians have with Christ that puts us in a deep, eternal relationship with one another."[18] It is God's Holy Spirit that unites us as believers. The most unlikely people gathered under one roof will have a supernatural connection with one another because they each have a personal relationship with Christ. They each reflect God's Spirit and, even though they may be divided on so many levels, they are one in Christ because Christ is central in each of them. They have the gift of God's Holy Spirit, Christ living in us, and that is the key to being able to engage in true worship with other believers. We are family with God as our Father. It is a most glorious miracle to see ex-cons, former adulterers, reformed liars, and ex-addicts come together with all of us other sinners in Christ's family with genuine love—sinners who, by the way, Jesus called saints! Adrian Rogers said, "Get everybody to love Jesus, and you've got a wonderful church. They don't have to

---

17. A. W. Tozer, *The Purpose of Man: Designed to Worship,* compiled and edited by James Snyder (Grand Rapids, MI: *Baker Books,* 2009) 50–51.

18. John Piper, "We Need Each Other: Christian Fellowship as a Means of Perservance," Heb. 3:12-14, (April 19, 2017), from desiringgod.org.

agree on anything else."[19] We saints are all sinners who have been forgiven of our sins by the grace of God. Romans 8:27 (ESV) says, "And he who searches hearts knows what is the mind of the Spirit, because the Spirit intercedes for the *saints* according to the will of God" (emphasis added). There are many other scripture references to God's children being called saints—not in the way the world sees that word, which is sinless without fault, but as redeemed children of God.

Are you a true saint? Or are you pretending to fit in God's family? Ever wear shoes that were too tight, and you had to use force to actually get your foot to fit in the shoe? Ouch! How uncomfortable! And it won't be long before you will be complaining and snapping at anyone who crosses your path because you are in pain. Could that describe how church worship feels to you? Can't wait to get home and kick it off and go back to your old ways? You may need to examine your heart to see if you are of the household of faith.

Think about what this verse is implying about how we should live our lives: "Those who say they live in God [are saved] should live as Jesus did" (1 John 2:6). That couldn't be clearer. Are we, then, to be perfect as Jesus was? He is to be our standard, and we can strive for perfection and be grateful for however things turn out from there. For the Bible also tells us we are to imitate God as dear children. What a sweet picture! We've all seen little boys putting on their dad's big boots and trying to walk in them. They do a clumsy job of it, but the reason they are in those boots in the first place is because they love Daddy and want to be like him. In the same way, we will be clumsy at best as we try to imitate our Father. Yet the reason we even try to do so in the first place is because we love Him and want to be like Him.

Why do we exercise? We do so to stay in shape and to become strong and revived physically as well as emotionally. Exercise stirs our blood and causes life-giving oxygen to be fed to every part of our body. You may have noticed that exercise

---

19. Adrian Rogers, *Adrianisms: The Wit and Wisdom of Adrian Rogers* (Memphis, TN: Love Worth Finding Ministries, 2006) 137.

feels uncomfortable when we first begin because it requires a bit of effort and determination. But as our muscles begin to move, we are rejuvenated, and our range of motion is greatly increased. Although there is some pain in pushing ourselves, our spirit is eager to get up the next day and do it again for our good. So it is with genuine worship.

Why worship? How is worship beneficial to our souls? Worship has the ability to transform our battered and bewildered souls. It has the power to change whatever bleak or hurtful perspective this nonsensical sinful world has thrust on us during the week. Worship gives us a new and hopeful perspective on how to navigate our day-in and day-out lives. This world is such a wicked place, filling us with discouragement, anxiety, even fear. But true worship of God *redirects our focus.* When we think on things above, we see God the Father seated on His throne and God the Son seated at His right hand. And we remember the gift of the Holy Spirit. With the Trinity in our heavenly sights, our troubled minds find a respite from all the baggage we've been forced to carry. We are able to leave all the things that have burdened us during the week—all the things that have worried us or frightened us or caused us alarm—at the feet of Jesus. Pure and simple worship of God gives a blessed relief, feeding life to our spiritually dry hearts, and we can feel strengthened as we lift our voices, our hands, and our hearts in praise to God. When we come to worship with a heart posture of gratitude, repentance, and devotion, our worship will be a sweet refreshment to our furrowed brows and aching hearts. We should never neglect the opportunity to worship the One who loves us with an unfailing love, for it is indeed a privilege, a necessity, and a delight.

Read the words of this lovely old hymn written by Helen H. Lemmel, "Turn Your Eyes Upon Jesus."

> Pure and simple worship of God gives a blessed relief, feeding life to our spiritually dry hearts, and we can feel strengthened as we lift our voices, our hands, and our hearts in praise to God.

O soul, are you weary and troubled?
No light in the darkness you see.
There's light for a look at the Savior
And life more abundant and free.

Turn your eyes upon Jesus.
Look full in His wonderful face.
And the things of earth will grow strangely dim
In the light of His glory and grace.

Therefore God has highly exalted Him [Jesus] and bestowed on Him the name that is above every name so that at the name of Jesus every knee should bow, in heaven and on earth and under the earth, and every tongue confess that Jesus Christ is Lord, to the glory of God the Father. (Phil. 2:9-11 ESV)

EXAMINE YOURSELF

When you read scripture, does it feel like it was written personally to you? Do its words grip your heart, causing you to examine your life? It should! Or do you worship with a condemning heart as others worship in truth?

Are you "looking for the back door?" Or do you rejoice in your soul because you're with the body of Christ?

God is patient and loving, always pursuing us into having a personal relationship with Him. The Bible was written just for you because Christ died just for you!

Chapter 9

PERSONAL RELATIONSHIP

No longer do I call you servants, for the servant does not know what his master is doing; but I have called you friends, for all that I have heard from my Father I have made known to you.
—John 15:15 (ESV)

If you ever attended an evangelical church, you most likely have heard that to be saved means we have a *personal relationship* with Jesus. And that's true. To have a personal relationship with God means that first, we must accept His free gift of salvation by repenting, dying to ourselves, and turning to Him. As Christ followers we are not our own. Scripture tells us we were bought for a price—the blood of Jesus our Redeemer. Those who have a personal relationship with God will include God in their daily lives, not just when trouble hits home. They pray to Him, read His Word, and meditate on verses in an effort to get to know Him even better. Jesus is the One who loved us enough to give

> **Those who have a personal relationship with God will include God in their daily lives, not just when trouble hits home.**

His life for us, and He is the One who bridged the gap between us and God. Christ's shed blood was our only hope.

A good example of having a personal relationship with Christ is to imagine the personal relationship between a child and her earthly father. Both know each other intimately in that they know each other's likes and dislikes. The child tells him her secrets and trusts that they're safe with Dad. When she is afraid, without any hesitation, she leaps into her father's arms for his strong protection. He sees his child when she cries and dries her tears, and his heart breaks with each one that falls. He laughs at her silly ways and loves to play games with her, and he blindsides her often with lovely gifts she neither expected nor deserved. His child instinctively knows that if her dad sees that she has a need, it is as good as done. Whatever it takes to fix her child-sized problems, Dad is there in a heartbeat. There is nothing this father will not do for her because she is his own, his blood. He loves his child more than life itself. But his love for his child never gives in to her foolish whims, which could ultimately harm her or spoil her. Her father would willingly give his life blood if needed. This describes a relationship between a child and her father and mimics what a personal relationship with God the Father looks like. Intimacy. Love. Teaching. Sacrificing. Delight. Trust. Faithfulness. Obedience.

It could be that some people don't understand what "personal relationship" means, especially in today's culture where healthy relationships are short-lived or nonexistent. It has become normal to live with someone until it no longer works. There's no commitment, so there's no need for explanation. Many in today's generation prefer as little personal contact with people as possible. They text, tweet, order online, email, or leave voicemails. Here we see a devastatingly effective weapon employed by Satan. His ways are subtle but lethal. He uses distrust, pain of past experiences, and the belief that there is no better way than to keep people isolated, making them vulnerable to his lies.

But there *is* a better way! For those of us who have had the beautiful gift of a personal relationship with someone we love, how would we say it can be characterized? Communication and a loving presence. My husband and I have our own separate routines each day, but each one is filled with "I love yous" and conversations and exchanges over a cup of coffee. We share our concerns with each other as well as what makes us happy. We hold hands, exchange a quick kiss, and embrace. Can you imagine a marriage where there was no communication or loving presence? What does it convey when these two elements are absent? It shows that there's little concern about what the other is feeling, thinking, or experiencing. It shows a lack of love and compassion or a desire to grow closer. A marriage without communication and loving presence is doomed because it lacks a relationship that is intimate and close. Genesis 1:26-27 tells us that God made us in His image. He created us to be like Him for relationship. A personal relationship with God is the most important relationship you will ever have. God made us for Himself, to enjoy us and fellowship with us and for us to be able to do the same with our Creator.

The Bible tells us that God desires us to have fellowship with Him and with each other. In the book of Isaiah, Abraham was called God's friend. What did that mean? Abraham loved God to the point of complete obedience to Him. But Abraham was more than an acquaintance with God. He was more than a companion to God. God called Abraham His friend because of the endearing and devoted relationship they had. God wants to call us His friend too.

It is through personal relationships that families succeed, that lifetime friends are made, and, not surprisingly, how we are to reach the lost. When we shut our eyes to why it's important to attend church and connect with other believers, when we shun developing close friendships with other Christians, we are allowing Satan, the god of this world (2 Cor. 4:4), to manipulate our minds and thus our future. There is an old story that talks about the hot glowing embers of a campfire. We see the power in the fiery coals that are clustered together as it brightens the night and warms the campsite. But then we can pull out just one ember that is glowing orange with heat, and before our very eyes we watch that one ember slowly fade out and cool, becoming, in essence, ineffective and useless.

God knew this about human nature before we did. That's why He tells us that we must develop close relationships with other Christians so that we can encourage one another, build up each other to finish the race, sympathize with and love one another, teach others, learn from others, and lovingly correct wrong ways. This is a picture of what God desires of us with Himself. A personal relationship with God requires time in prayer, in conversation with God. It requires time in reading His Word. It requires time of introspection and examination of ourselves to see whether our relationship with Him is as it ought to be. A personal relationship with God requires repentance, obedience, sacrifice and worship. Satan works at pulling believers out of the "campfire" so we can either burn out or not grow in our faith. And if he can keep us separate without having ever been "set afire," all the better! Then our spiritual eyes will remain closed to God's truth. Personal relationships with godly people and with God Himself is essential for spiritual understanding and growth.

So many in this entitled culture we are now living in are, not surprisingly, self-sufficient, self-deceived, self-centered, arrogant, unwilling to repent, and demanding of whatever it is they desire. They want all the blessings, their prayers to be heard and answered, and salvation from a God they will not make a commitment to. *A God they have no personal relationship with.* "A relationship with God simply cannot grow when money, sins, activities, favorite sport teams, addictions, or commitments are piled up on top of it."[20]

Sadly, many are choosing to *date* Jesus or have only a casual relationship with Him, maintaining their desire

---

20. Francis Chan, featured in Francis Chan Quotes on quotefancy.com (2023).

for freedom to live as they choose. They reject the idea of a commitment to love just Him. They've put themselves and worldly pleasures ahead of God. They proudly wear the badge of Christian, but their life doesn't reflect Jesus. Many will curse God as if they can manipulate Him and treat Him more like a doddering old man. I liken this to a bug crawling across the pavement, shaking his tiny fist at the one towering above it who has all power and authority to squash it at any time. The arrogance and ignorance of the creation toward the Creator is heartbreaking. Yet God's love for us is unfailing and unending. It is His merciful and gracious love that seeks each of us to come to Himself for forgiveness and salvation through the blood of Jesus. It has long been a personal question of mine as to why people avoid at all costs the One who offered His very life for theirs. Never will we find a greater, more sacrificial love than the love Jesus has for us. "A man will go to hell unsaved, but he will never go unloved."[21]

> It has long been a personal question of mine as to why people avoid at all costs the One who offered His very life for theirs. Never will we find a greater, more sacrificial love than the love Jesus has for us.

Having a personal relationship with Jesus Christ will give you a spiritual peace you can never know outside of Him. Loving Jesus in whom we have a personal relationship deepens our desire to open up ourselves, spilling our inmost emotions and fears, laying aside what burdens us or has us in chains, and lifting our eyes to Jesus. This kind of personal relationship with God allows us to let down our guard and agree with God that He is our all in all. The following story reveals the vulnerability of us all. But instead of falling into despair, God graced me with answered prayer. Why? Because our relationship is *personal*.

---

21. Adrian Rogers, *The Adrian Rogers Legacy Bible,* John 3:16,17 (Memphis, TN: Love Worth Finding Ministries, 2009) 1,190.

I BELIEVE IN GOD, SO I'M SAVED, RIGHT?

Oh No! What Have I Done?

In my distress I cried unto the Lord, and He heard me.
(Ps. 120:1 KJV)

Ever since my first stay in a bed and breakfast, I've wanted to open my own. We had never stayed in a B&B before. Somehow we heard about one in Brinkley, Arkansas, called the Great Southern. This was an old railroad station that had the first floor converted into a few rooms and a restaurant. I soon found myself longing to be the owner of my very own bed and breakfast. I loved the casual atmosphere and the mystique of a past era showcased in each room. The notion had stolen my heart!

So began our new type of weekend outing once we were back in Bartlett. For years we'd go on adventures to small towns we'd never explored before. We'd line up a real estate agent to show us house after house, and in so doing, we learned a lot about what it would mean to be the owners of an old house. Our initial questions were always, *How many layers of roof does it have? How old is the water heater? Are there any leaks? How old is the wiring?* These are things that would run off any intelligent buyer, but when you've been bitten by the old house bug and you're still young, prudence runs out the old screen door! So we found a house in Hickory Valley, Tennessee, that we loved. It was built in 1898 and was of Queen-Anne-Victorian-style architecture. At the time, the asking price was one hundred thousand dollars. That was more than we wanted to pay, so we bantered between ourselves about what we could offer. It was a wasted effort because someone else came along and offered five thousand dollars over the asking price. Seems they wanted it as badly as we did.

I was crushed. My friends knew about this dream I had of owning and running a B&B, and sometimes they'd stick a real estate ad in our mailbox for us to think about. I remember being so disheartened when I found a picture of a house that was for sale in my mailbox—a picture of a ranch-style house in a subdivision. I moaned that nobody knew what I wanted. Really? A ranch-style B&B? Time passed, and my husband and I continued to enjoy our weekend outings of visiting old homes in areas nearby because my husband would still be driving to school, teaching in Shelby County.

One day, back in the day when people read newspapers, my husband came running into the kitchen to find me. He looked so funny! His legs wouldn't straighten up—like Harpo Marx. He was so excited because he'd found a new listing in the paper in the real estate section. It was the Hickory Valley house!

We set up a time to see it. We couldn't believe what we saw. The first time we saw it, there were many expensive projects that needed to be done. But these new owners had, by the grace of God, repaired and restored things that we could have never afforded to do like they did. A bowed-out wall on the staircase had been sheet rocked and papered in tasteful Victorian-style wallpaper. In fact, other old plaster walls had been repaired and papered, making the rooms look clean and inviting. They'd even had smooth ceilings put in most rooms. Don't get me wrong, there were still plenty of projects, but they were ones we felt capable of attacking.

How exciting for me! And scary for my husband. There was not one corpuscle in me that didn't surge at the thought of getting this house up to snuff and then running it as an inn. My husband, on the other hand, wasn't as sure. Soon we were deep into renovation, painting, hanging drapes, laying new carpet, installing new toilets, painting porches. It was an endless list, but they were, to me, labors of love.

Not long after living there, we had not quite gotten things where we needed them to be as far as having overnight guests. So to generate some money in the meantime, I decided to offer a Valentine's Day lunch. What fun I had planning the menu, making napkins, polishing silver candle holders, and so forth. I

I BELIEVE IN GOD, SO I'M SAVED, RIGHT?

put an ad in the local paper. Now comes the part where I realized I didn't know a thing about starting a business.

A day or two after the ad came out in the paper, I got a call from the county health department. They'd seen our ad and had a few questions for me. Long story short, I was informed that in order to have food and guests I'd need a business license. No problem. But then they ripped out my heart. They wanted to know my plans for the future. I told them that owning and running a B&B had always been a dream of mine. That the house was once used as a bed and breakfast—for many years, in fact. I knew that because I'd seen postcards in the Chamber of Commerce in Bolivar for people to pick up. It had a picture of our old house on the front, advertising it as a B&B in Hickory Valley. The owners had even told us about all the interesting people who had stayed with them through the years. But the health department went on to tell me that the house had never had a license to be run as a B&B, so, since it was now many years later, 1997, there were new laws that would apply. I was told that I'd have to have a private bath built onto each bedroom that I intended to rent out. Also, for safety purposes, they gave me a list as long as my arm about proper fire exits, how all windows without screens had to be securely closed, the need for maps in each room showing an escape route in case of fire, proper ways to wash and shelve my dishes—all things that would make the health department happy. Everything they wanted I could provide. Except building the new baths. We simply could not afford to do that.

What were we going to do? We had made a huge leap of faith buying this home. We couldn't put more money into it now. We needed to open this inn now and start making some income, but our hands were tied. What was I going to tell my husband? He was an hour away, teaching a classroom full of fifth graders. He'd be coming home soon, worn out and frazzled. And I was going to have to dump this on him. This had been *my* dream, after all, and he was supporting me the best he could by simply agreeing to drive so far in to work every day. I was scared

PERSONAL RELATIONSHIP

and sick to my stomach. Had we bought a house we couldn't even afford to open as an inn?

But then . . . I went out on one of our many porches. I sat on the top wooden step and leaned back against an old porch post that had been there for a hundred years. The warm sun was bathing my face. I shut my eyes, but my mouth fell open as I wailed in my soul. *Oh, Lord, please help us!* I cried out loud. *What are we going to do?* It was the kind of crying we've all read about in the Bible. God tells us that there are times we don't even know how to pray. Where we don't even know what to say. And that's because we are so broken in spirit we cannot find the words. But God's Holy Spirit promises to intervene for us, and He takes our gut-wrenching utterances and puts meaning to them as He delivers our words to the Father. That was all I could do at that moment—pour out my pain in groanings to the Lord.

Then, I heard my phone ring. It was an old-fashioned landline because Hickory Valley couldn't even boast that they had a cell phone tower.

"Hello?"

"Mrs. Rogers? This is [so and so] from the county health department. We spoke with you this morning, remember?"

I was numb.

"We've decided after much discussion that, since your home used to be run as a bed and breakfast for so many years, and that there were postcards actually advertising it as a B&B, and even though there's never been a business license bought to use it for that purpose, we will allow you to run your inn as if it's always been licensed."

Next, the sound of my sobbing.

The health department never came onto our property after that. Never. But we at least learned how to run things safely and how to sanitize my kitchen space and dishes properly, among other necessary things. The Lord blessed us with five wonderful years of interesting people and many stories to tell. We made sure everyone who booked with us knew that their innkeepers were Christians and were delighted to share our wonderful home with them. Upstairs in the cozy sitting area for our guests was a folder with the printed story about how our inn came to be. I wanted everyone to know how God miraculously intervened. Many of our guests were Christians as well, and they'd remark how much they enjoyed their stay with us and hoped to return someday. Many of them did. It was our hope that each of them took our miracle story and shared it with others. God blessed me by giving me my impossible dream come true.

Across from the inn's driveway is an old building that once was a general store. The previous owners of the inn were also Christians, and the wife was an artist. She had painted the most attractive mural on the exterior old brick wall along with the words, "Whatever you do, do it all for the glory of God (1 Cor. 10:31)." The Avent-Rogers Bed and Breakfast was surely for His glory. And we were blessed beyond measure.

In the first section of this book we learned about the word *believe* and touched on the personal aspect of that word. Christ died for the sins of the world, but more importantly, Christ died for *your* sins. His death was very personal. And because He made that sacrifice just for you, you must personally decide what you're going to do with that.

EXAMINE YOURSELF

How do you personally feel when a commitment to you is broken or not taken seriously?

What is holding you back from making a total commitment of your life to Jesus? Look at the cross and realize His commitment to you was 100%, and He deserves no less.

PERSONAL RELATIONSHIP

To have a passing thought of Jesus is not a relationship; it's merely an acknowledgment of His existance. What burdens are you carrying that you need to place in God's capable hands?

Realize that in spite of the sinful and rebellious people we are, Christ desires to have a personal relationship with us. He created you for Himself. Do you desire a personal relationship with Jesus? Repent, ask for God's forgiveness, and surrender your life to His lordship. He loves you!

Have you felt betrayal in the past with people who you trusted and fear rejection again? Jesus promises to never leave you nor forsake you because He is faithful even when we aren't.

How would your life be different if Christ was your personal Lord and Master? Are you in need of a changed, transformed life? Jesus offers a new life to those who choose to follow Him in loving obedience.

Chapter 10

This is my commandment: Love each other in the same way I have loved you. There is no greater love than to lay down one's life for one's friends.
—John 15:12-13

I love old black-and-white movies. Many love a good steak or a hot cup of coffee. But then there are those amazing grandkids that we love! We may love a certain color or even a certain person. But these examples have nothing to do with the type of love we are commanded to have as Christ followers. These are all a natural type of love that anyone can enjoy. But there is nothing *supernatural* about any of these types of love. Christ loves us with a supernatural love that we are called to imitate as Christians.

You may think this chapter is going to be all sugar and spice and everything nice. But love is a huge component identifying us with Christ—a kind of love that may be quite painful in the process. It's not just any kind of love but the kind of love Jesus showed the world. Sacrificial love. Love that is willing to go to any length to reach the lost and hurting. Do you display this kind of agape love? The introductory verse to this chapter is from the very lips of our Savior: "This is my commandment: Love each other in the same way I have loved you." You may ask, *In what way did He love?* As we study that question, please take time to search your heart to see if the love of Jesus abides in you. As simple as it would seem to be, to "love," in this case, can only be accomplished by the presence of the Holy Spirit in our life. To obey this command of Christ's involves dying to self and having a very *intentional* aim to *love and serve others as He did.* Yes, loving and serving others and giving of ourselves are interlocked with one another. They are two sides of the same coin. Pastor Adrian Rogers said you can give without loving, but you can't love without giving.[22]

> To obey this command of Christ's involves dying to self and having a very *intentional* aim to *love and serve others as He did.*

Any kind-hearted person can perform a good deed for someone. Haven't we all experienced a stranger helping us with a flat tire or bringing us fresh produce from their garden? Friendliness of this nature is so appreciated because, these days, it seems we don't see very many people taking the time to be nice. But realize that just doing someone a kindness without the love of Jesus in us as our motivation has no eternal or lasting value. Woodrow Kroll is an evangelical preacher and hosted at one time the international radio ministry called "Back to the Bible." Every day that I heard his program, he would always close out with these words that have stuck with me all these many years: "Have a good and godly day. For of what lasting value is a good day if it is not also a godly day?"[23] Matthew 5:16 (NASB) says, "In the same way, let your good deeds shine out for all to see, so that everyone will praise your heavenly Father." Serving in the name

---

22. Adrian Rogers, *Adrianisms: The Wit and Wisdom of Adrian Rogers* (Memphis, TN: Love Worth Finding Ministries, 2006) 142.

23. Woodrow Kroll, closing line in his "Back to the Bible" international radio ministry.

of Jesus is the opposite of serving for recognition and praise from man. Our good deeds or our *light* is to always point people to Jesus. Our highest praise will be this: May we so live to enjoy that day when the Lord may say to us, "Well done, thou good and faithful servant" (Matt. 25:21 KJV).

Let us first explore the different kinds of love so we may focus on the one we are to exhibit as Christians. *Phileo* love is a naturally occurring kind of love. It's a kind of love that expresses warm affection and friendship. You may know that the city of Philadelphia has been nicknamed the "City of Brotherly Love." That's because in the Greek language, *phileo* means brotherly love.

Eros love is the physical intimacy between a husband and wife in marriage. Yes, *eros* love is a gift from God. If you have ever read Song of Solomon in the Bible, you may be surprised at the strong imagery of two young married lovers. The scripture gives us vivid mental pictures that can make some people blush. On the other hand, because of wickedness in the world, we all have been overexposed and sickened by man's perversion of this *eros* type of love as it is depicted outside of the divine confines of marriage. Pornography is an example as well as sex trafficking. But let's not overlook what has become acceptable in our society today, including extramarital affairs, living together before marriage, and the like. God has a specific design for sex, which He gave as a gift to those who love Him and even those who don't. And when an *eros* type of love is used in a way outside of God's plan of marriage, it is sin.

Our understanding of *agape* love is different in many ways. First, *agape* love is a sacrificial love, an unconditional love originating with God. Whereas the world's love is characterized by selfishness. Apart from the power of the Holy Spirit in our lives, we are incapable of showing *agape* love. This is a divine love. Apart from God, we are selfish and love ourselves more than others. Scripture shows us characteristics that God gifts us with when we are saved. We are given love, joy, peace, patience, kindness, goodness, faithfulness, gentleness, and self-control when Christ is our Savior. When we love like Jesus, we see beyond ourselves and see the needs of others. We can throw off the cloak of selfishness, resentment, anxiety, pettiness, and entitlement.

As an example of this supernatural gift of God's love, let me share a personal story that still to this day amazes me. It's a story about a most unlikely friendship. It's a story of loving someone as I watched them slowly die. And it's a story of God's amazing love in bringing two people together who would have otherwise never met.

Marilyn

> *"I was sick and you visited Me. . . . Truly, I say to you, as you did it to one of the least of these, my brothers, you did it to Me." (Matt. 25:35-45 ESV)*

That's all of her name that I know. Marilyn. I used to have her last name on a tiny slip of paper, but that's long gone. The memories, however, of an incredible and mysterious friendship that the Lord blessed me with, are not lost.

I was living in Whiteville, Tennessee, at the time I met Marilyn. I was putting on my makeup like every other morning when I began to feel like I was needed . . . somewhere. Or was it that I was the one in need? I began to pray as I continued to apply blush that the Lord would show me what it was I was feeling. I had a deep empty feeling. I felt like there was something very necessary and urgent that the Lord wanted me to do. Maybe. I just wasn't sure. So there I was that morning, with half a face of makeup, wondering where this day was going.

I finished the task at hand and got dressed. I'd been mulling it over in my mind that perhaps someone needed a visit. Who would that be? I remembered the nursing home nearby. I didn't personally know anyone who was staying there, but I knew its halls were full of old souls thirsty for conversation. So I decided to go there and do just that.

As I was driving down Highway 64, I was still inquiring of the Lord. And I was straining to hear Him. Where was this car going? Who would I meet? There was no mistaking that God was orchestrating something for me that day—I just didn't know what.

I opened the doors to the nursing home and was met by empty stares of people who once were vibrant, hardworking citizens. They had lives that had been blessed with children, husbands and wives, homes and vacations, jobs and celebrations, just like me. But their days were fading now, and they barely resembled who they once were. It was one of these people the Lord wanted me to meet. Maybe to be a blessing to.

I went to the nurses' station and simply said, "I don't know any resident here, but the Lord spoke to my heart this morning, and I feel there's someone who needs a visit . . . who needs encouragement." Without hesitation, two nurses looked at each other and said in unison, "Marilyn." Wow! God had already chosen! They told me that she wasn't from around here. That she was from Memphis, and she didn't have any relatives or friends that visited because they were all out of town. She only had a brother who lived in another state who seldom visited. But they failed to tell me just how close to the end of her life she was.

I've never known anyone who was in the process of dying. I didn't even know what it looked like, so when I found Marilyn, I wasn't thinking it was the end. She was dying of cancer of some kind. She looked normal to me except she was skeletal. She smiled and seemed to comprehend what was going on. In fact, she was even near my age! I had expected a much older person. As we visited, I told her about myself, and she told me about herself. What was most peculiar was that we had so much in common. I had told her I was a seamstress for a decorator. She had been a decorator and sewed as well. So we understood fabric and design and colors and decorating. Then she told me that she grew up near Eastgate Shopping Center and the Memphis State area. So did I! So we were able to talk about the old days. We actually had quite a jaunty visit! I told her I'd be back, and I was. Several times.

One day when I returned, she wasn't there. They told me she'd been admitted to the hospital next door. I didn't ask what the problem was. When I located her room, I went in and discovered a "different" Marilyn. She was talking pretty normally except that she was very demanding. Agitated. She asked if I would leave and bring back some ginger ale made with "real" ginger. I left and had to go to a couple of stores before I found a bottle of Canada Dry Ginger Ale—the kind with real ginger. She said she had such a craving for real ginger ale, and I certainly wanted to oblige. When I went back to her room, she was very pushy!

"Open it now and put it in this cup. No, I don't want that much! Just a little!"

The nurse came in and saw the party that was going on and informed me that she wasn't supposed to be drinking that. Well, I had quite a struggle on my hands as I attempted to take away her cup. What a comical scene ensued! It's hard to talk mean to someone you know is dying. Anyway, later that week she was moved back to the nursing home.

It was around Thanksgiving, and I remember presidential elections were going on. When the nurse came in to check on something, I asked her what kind of meds Marilyn took because I never saw any being administered. She told me that she was on no medication at all. Like I said previously, she was skeletal with a distended stomach. I'm sure anyone who knows anything about nursing would have immediately realized that she was near death. She was at the point of not even having pain.

I continued visiting her every day. I brought her things for her room—things to hang on her wall, lotion to rub on her feet and hands. She showed me her nails that a volunteer had done the day before, and she was so proud.

LOVE

On what was to be my last visit, I went to her usual room at the nursing home, and her bed was made. That scared me. But the front desk told me she was in another room just down the hall. Again, I was not told that she had been moved there to die. I walked in, and she was either asleep or in a coma. I never knew. But I soon realized what was going on. I pulled a chair up to her bedside as close as I could get to her ear, and I spoke softly to her words of comfort—that I loved her and that God loved her. I had already talked to her about her salvation experience. She had repented and asked the Lord to save her many years back and was not afraid of dying at all. She looked forward to seeing Jesus. I stayed about forty-five minutes that day. I prayed in her ear and asked that God would take care of her. I thanked God for bringing us together. Then I left.

The next day I went to the same private room to see her. It was empty. They told me she passed away about ten minutes after I left the day before. Just think . . . angels were poised to escort Marilyn to heaven when I had been there.

I found out where her service was going to be. It wouldn't be normal because of the few people that she knew. My husband drove me to the funeral home that evening for the visitation. In fact, I believe that's the only service there was. I went in, and there were two people standing by the casket. It was Marilyn's brother and his wife. They were shocked to see anyone coming in because as far as they knew, Marilyn had no living friends. I introduced myself to them and explained my relationship with Marilyn. She had told me in one of our visits that her brother and his wife were not believers. That explained their suspicion. I saw it in their eyes, and their words were very measured. Especially when I mentioned that the Lord spoke to my heart to find her. I knew they couldn't understand how God could speak to an unknown person's heart and lead them to a dying woman who needed a friend. They couldn't understand how a virtual stranger could have tears in her eyes because she loved his sister. They were lost about everything.

I BELIEVE IN GOD, SO I'M SAVED, RIGHT?

A day is surely coming when I too will get to go home. Marilyn and I will see each other, and I'll finally get a chance to point my finger at her and say, "What was up that day about the ginger ale?"

Thank You, Lord, for a chance to "do unto You."

What you just read is not a *natural* kind of love. There is no way I could have loved this woman as I did without God's Spirit being within me. It's only by the power of God's divine *agape* kind of love we can love the unlovable and see them through the eyes of Jesus. How else do we explain how we can forgive people who've hurt us without cause? How else can we explain why we will stop in the middle of Walmart and pray for someone we see is hurting? What about those times we've given money that could have been used to pay our bills or buy our groceries, but instead our hearts led us to give what we had to another in need? And in each instance, we do it in the name of Jesus, for His glory alone and not ours. What about organizations like Samaritan's Purse or Sunday school teachers or those annoying people who hand out gospel tracts? Why are they doing what they do? How are they doing what they do? Missionaries put their lives and the lives of their families on the line. What drives them? Visiting homeless shelters in the inner cities—why would men, women, boys, and girls devote their time to ride a bus for an hour just to serve a meal and minister to these lonely souls? The only explanation is God in us! *Is the love of God in you?*

> *Then the King will say to those on his right, "Come, you who are blessed by my Father, inherit the Kingdom prepared for you from the creation of the world. For I was hungry, and you fed me. I was thirsty, and you gave me a drink. I was a stranger, and you invited*

> There is no way I could have loved this woman as I did without God's Spirit being within me. It's only by the power of God's divine *agape* kind of love we can love the unlovable and see them through the eyes of Jesus.

me into your home. I was naked, and you gave me clothing. I was sick, and you cared for me. I was in prison, and you visited me." Then these righteous ones will reply, "Lord, when did we ever see you hungry and feed you? Or thirsty and give you something to drink? Or a stranger and show you hospitality? Or naked and give you clothing? When did we ever see you sick or in prison and visit you?" And the King will say, "I tell you the truth, when you did it to one of the least of these my brothers and sisters, you were doing it to me!" Then the King will turn to those on the left and say, "Away with you, you cursed ones, into the eternal fire prepared for the devil and his demons. For I was hungry, and you didn't feed me. I was thirsty, and you didn't give me a drink. I was a stranger, and you didn't invite me into your home. I was naked, and you didn't give me clothing. I was sick and in prison, and you didn't visit me." Then they will reply, "Lord, when did we ever see you hungry or thirsty or a stranger or naked or sick or in prison, and not help you?" And he will answer, "I tell you the truth, when you refused to help the least of these my brothers and sisters, you were refusing to help me." And they will go away into eternal punishment, but the righteous will go into eternal life. (Matt. 25:34-46)

Many see love as only an emotion, but the kind of love God has for us and has given us by His Spirit is more than an emotion. It is the identity of a true believer. God is love. Scripture tells us that we are to imitate Him as dear children. To say you are a Christian and not have love in your heart for others is an oxymoron. Remember, God sent His one and only Son to die a criminal's death on a cross for *our* sake. Yours and mine. And until we receive God's forgiveness of our sin, we too are also offensive to God and an enemy of His. Those of us who are off-put by the inconveniences, the ugly, rude, addicted, entitled, foul-mouthed, mentally ill, ignorant and uneducated, and most of all needy people we encounter every day, consider we are no different from the very ones we ourselves shun. Yet, while we were still sinners, or you might say "needy," Christ died for us. Mark 10:45 tells us, "For even the Son of Man came not to be served, but to serve, and to give His life as a ransom for many." What amazing love!

Are you familiar with what is called the "love chapter" in the Bible? First Corinthians 13 describes the futility and uselessness of a life lived without love.

> *If I could speak all the languages of earth and of angels, but didn't love others, I would only be a noisy gong or a clanging cymbal. If I had the gift of prophesy and if I understood all of God's secret plans and possessed all knowledge, and if I had such faith that I could move mountains, but didn't love others, I would be nothing. If I gave everything I have to the poor and even sacrificed my body, I could boast about it, but if I didn't love others, I would have gained nothing. Love is patient and kind. Love is not jealous or boastful or proud or rude. It does not demand its own way. It is not irritable and it keeps no record of being wronged. It does not rejoice about injustice but rejoices whenever the truth wins out. Love never gives up, never loses faith, is always hopeful and endures through every circumstance. . . . Three things will last forever—faith, hope, and love—and the greatest of these is love. (1 Cor. 13:1-7, 13)*

Like the beloved Christmas movie "The Grinch that Stole Christmas," perhaps we need to see if we even have a heart. To know Jesus is to love.

EXAMINE YOURSELF

How have you personally shown someone you love them?

How can you improve on displaying a Christ-like agape love to your neighbors, friends, and family?

When did you last experience agape love from someone? Why was it meaningful to you?

Do you wonder why we must love? First John 4:7-9 (NIV) says, "Dear friend, let us love one another, for love comes from God. Everyone who loves has been born of God and knows God. Whoever does not love does not know God, because God is love. This is how God showed his love among us: He sent his one and only Son into the world that we might live through him."

Chapter 11

WITNESS

But you will receive power when the Holy Spirit comes upon you. And you will be my witnesses, telling people about Me everywhere—in Jerusalem, throughout Judea, in Samaria, and to the ends of the earth.
—Acts 1:8

Jesus tells us that we are to be His witnesses to people everywhere. So what does it mean to be a *witness*? This is in the same family as *testimony* but a bit broader. Our testimony focuses primarily on our personal story of salvation where *witness* is meant to touch or influence lives for Christ in our community and even beyond.

You may automatically think of the Jehovah's Witnesses. Sadly, many times they are the only witnesses we've ever met. This is sad for two reasons. The first is there are not nearly enough Christians bold enough to answer the call of Acts 1:8. This is the duty of all Christendom to spread the Good News about Jesus! It is the truth of God found within the pages of our Bible that we are to share with a spiritually dying world. Romans

1:16 (ESV) tells us, "For I am not ashamed of the gospel, for it is the power of God for salvation to everyone who believes, to the Jew first and also the Greek." The second reason it is sad is because Jehovah's Witness is a false religion—yet some of their methods are to be admired and appreciated. They go out into neighborhoods in pairs, knocking on every door, ready to give the homeowner a brochure of their beliefs as written by the Watch Tower Society along with a friendly, albeit sometimes intense, conversation. It may have the sound of truth to it and may have a somewhat familiar ring as well; however, if you are already a Christian and are familiar with your Bible the way you should be, you'll quickly pick up on this false doctrine. This is called godly discernment, and the Holy Spirit gives it to each of us who believe. "Discernment is not knowing the difference between right and wrong. It is knowing the difference between right and *almost* right."[24] A parachute that *almost* works is a tragedy. There are just some things where *almost* is not enough. People need biblical truth that is solid because *almost truth* is a lie.

You may have heard of EE—Evangelism Explosion. This is a Christian evangelistic ministry and training program that has proven to be highly effective in winning people to Jesus using everyday Christians who have been given the tools to equip others for this task. But I think ultimately there is no better method of being a witness of Jesus Christ than the good old-fashioned, two-way conversation within a casual setting using whatever opportunity God has just put in our lap. First Peter 3:15 says, "And if someone asks about your hope as a believer, always be ready to explain it." Colossians 4:5-6 says, "Live wisely among those who are not believers and make the most of every opportunity."

I can't even begin to tell you how many times God has opened a door so wide for me to say a word on behalf of His Son that I had no choice but to walk through it. God recognizes

---

24. C. H. Spurgeon, in article by CeCe Burger Sharpe entitled, "Considering the Difference between Right and Almost Right," from Theriverbendgroup.com (September 24, 2021).

a heart that is willing to be used. It may not be a heart that is wholly confident in itself or one that is overly eager to jump into the unknown, but God promises to use those who make themselves available to Him. He also promises to give us words in our mouths and to bring to memory what we need to say. But let's not misinterpret this like the praying student in class taking a test he did not prepare for. We need to already know what God's Word says. Then He will bring to mind those powerful words for His glory.

> God recognizes a heart that is willing to be used. It may not be a heart that is wholly confident in itself or one that is overly eager to jump into the unknown, but God promises to use those who make themselves available to Him.

Has someone ever witnessed to you? What was your response? If you were an unbeliever, I'm pretty sure you were irritated, if not angry. Probably because you saw this selfless act as being judgmental. Could it be that God sent that person to you to give you some hope for your future? Could it be that your life displays a life that doesn't know Jesus personally? I've been in the same shoes as you then. And I've also been in the same shoes as the one sharing the gospel.

I remember being at a mall in Memphis so long ago as a young woman. I was sitting on an indoor brick wall, waiting on my friend to come out of a store. I had seen who I considered *old* people walking the mall briskly and paid little attention to them. Suddenly an old man diverted his path straight to me! He quickly handed me a tract about salvation and with no words continued on his walk. I was startled but also offended. *How dare him think I needed that tract! How dare he single me out of all these other people!* Let me explain now, in hindsight, what actually happened. At that time in my life, I was not a Christian. I *thought* I was, which is why I was offended. I knew that God existed, but that was all. I now know that this man was being used by God Himself. This one man obeyed God who had His holy eye on me, a lost young woman who had no thought of her eternity. Out of all the people at the mall that night, God chose *me* to receive the truth about His Son, Jesus, and His salvation. Realize also that this happened fifty-plus years ago, and I still remember it like it was yesterday. That unknown older man had just planted a seed in my heart that God would grow. Here I am today, sharing the same Good News with you because that seed took root! How very blessed I was that God loved me so much that He orchestrated this very simple encounter. When I get to heaven I'm going to look up this man and thank him for stepping outside his comfort zone to hand me words of life!

When we hear about someone's passing, do we wonder if they were a Christian or not? How tragic to have had an opportunity to share the salvation that only Jesus can offer and not do it. Could our witness have made a difference in their life? We may never know until we ourselves are standing in heaven. Will we see them?

I have a new way of looking at witnessing since I've grown in my knowledge of the Bible and God. I used to be terrified that the person I was speaking to would become angry or upset with me. How awful to think that how I thought they'd think about *me* would prevent them from hearing how to have eternal life! Is there anything more selfish? I was more concerned about myself at that moment than where they would spend eternity. Dr. Charles Stanley said, "Obey God and leave the consequences to Him."[25] Believing those words will lift the burden from off your shoulders. I still have those thoughts that someone may not appreciate hearing about Jesus, but whether they realize it or not, I'm thrilled to think that I've just shared with them something that could change the whole course of their life. Like the man at the mall did for me.

Witnessing can be as simple as speaking to someone at the gas pumps, asking whether they attend church somewhere or not. Then, depending upon their reply, you follow up with an invitation to your church or tell them that Jesus loves them. I have simple cards printed up to hand out at a moment's notice

---

25. Dr. Charles Stanley, *30 Life Principles Study Guide* (Nashville, TN: In Touch Ministries, Thomas Nelson Publishers, 2008).

for occasions just like this one. One card says, "Good News" with a couple of verses about Jesus and salvation. Since it's entitled "Good News," it's so easy to walk up to a person anywhere, in a store, at a desk, on the street, hand them the card and say, "I have some Good News for you!" Without exception, everyone smiles and takes the card because they're probably thinking I've just handed them a gift card! They always say, "Thank you," but by then I'm well on my way, praising God that another seed has just been planted. Even if they throw it down, someone may pick it up and receive the same blessing.

Why does God call us to share the gospel with others? Isn't that the job for paid preachers? As you read these following verses, think about the times people cared enough to share with you how to be saved: "How will they call on Him in whom they have not believed? And how are they to believe in Him of whom they have never heard? And how are they to hear without someone preaching? And how are they to preach unless they are sent? As it is written, 'How beautiful are the feet of those who preach the good news!'" (Rom. 10:14-15 ESV). And before we become defensive, saying that we are not preachers, understand this. The word *preach* comes from the Greek word *kerusso*, which means to proclaim, to declare, to announce, or to herald a message. Yes, we are all called to preach the Good News. What a privilege!

In the book of Ezekiel, we find a prophet who was tempted, at times, to keep quiet about sharing God's messages to the people of Israel. Does it sound strange that a prophet would be so disappointed in how God's message was being received that he'd consider saying nothing? After all, he was just a man chosen by God to speak to His people about repentance. God knows our hearts, and He knew Ezekiel's. Listen to what God told him:

> *Once again a message came to me from the Lord: "Son of man, give your people this message: 'When I bring an army against a country, the people of that land choose one of their own to be a watchman. When the watchman sees the enemy coming, he sounds the alarm to warn the*

> *people. Then if those who hear the alarm refuse to take action, it is their own fault if they die. They heard the alarm but ignored it, so the responsibility is theirs. If they had listened to the warning, they could have saved their lives. But if the watchman sees the enemy coming and doesn't sound the alarm to warn the people, he is responsible for their captivity. They will die in their sins, but I will hold the watchman responsible for their deaths.' Now, son of man, I am making you a watchman for the people of Israel." (Ezek. 33:1-7)*

As soldiers of the Lord, we have a grave responsibility to warn people about the enemy and to sound the alarm so they can be saved. We too are watchmen called by God to herald the Good News that Jesus Christ saves.

> **We too are watchmen called by God to herald the Good News that Jesus Christ saves.**

I'm excited to share two personal stories from my life that involve witnessing. They are two very different depictions but equally amazing. Please pay attention to the fact that in each story, I am such a weak vessel being used. Nervous, shy, and completely relying on the Holy Spirit to see me through. I am no different from you or any other person. But when you have made Jesus your very own, nothing we do after that makes much sense—at least to the world. When God is "in us," powerful and amazing things will fill your life.

Being in the World, Not of the World

> *He said to me, "My grace is sufficient for you, for my power is made perfect in weakness." Therefore I will boast all the more gladly about my weaknesses, so that the power of Christ may rest on me. (2 Cor. 12:9 NIV)*

I hate the way fear makes me feel, don't you? My symptoms include a knot in my stomach, trembling knees, sweaty hands, a shaky voice, dry mouth, and a brain that has come to a standstill. These leave a person feeling totally out of control. I used to suffer terribly with anxiety, but with prayer, good advice from a psychologist, and a commitment to not let it take over my life, I no longer am a prisoner to it. But still, fear creeps in. When we forget that it is in our *weaknesses* that the Lord is best able to show His power, we will always feel inadequate. And if we're not careful, we will turn back without ever attempting what God has placed before us, leaving us to wonder what could have been.

Every time I drove down the highway, I passed a dilapidated bar. Layers of peeling paint had a very unwelcoming feel. Yet the flashing arrow on the portable sign promised the opposite: "Open—Drinks tonight! 2 for 1!" During the day I'd only seen one car there, probably belonging to the owner who lived there. I had no idea who that might be. But in the evening at dusk, that flashing arrow was a beacon, luring customers off the side of the road.

It looked sleazy. It looked seedy. Yet people were drawn to it for whatever hope it held for them. It saddened me to think of the tired husband, the barely-of-age young boy, or the woman who might be sitting inside when I drove past. Was it the alcohol they needed? Was it a place of refuge and fellowship for some? I could only wonder. I knew, however, it wasn't a place I wanted to go to.

One day I realized that I'd been driving past the bar on a regular basis. How dare I not be concerned about the spiritual welfare of those who were inside. No, it wasn't a place I'd usually stop by, but for some reason, the Lord caused my heart to lock onto the hopelessness that was inside. I decided to gather together a bag of tempting treats. Everyone loves gifts of food. I always like using food as a way to step inside someone's life. It's simple and kind and non-threatening. So I packed a bag with cheese, grapes, deli ham, a loaf of fresh baked bread, olives, nuts, and gourmet cookies. At the last minute, I dropped a Christian CD inside. Probably a tract on how to be saved, and a note inviting them to visit our church. It was a pretty day when I decided to stop. I got out and walked to the dark mouth of the cave. At least that's how it felt. It was morning, and I wasn't sure if the bar was open yet since there were no cars outside. So I knocked. I could see inside as I peered through a screen door. There was nobody to be seen. Finally, a frazzled-looking woman came out of a side room and cautiously walked toward me. I introduced myself before she even got to the door so she'd know I wasn't a threat. She opened the screen door and stepped out on the gravel stoop with me.

May I say that it was about here when I thought for sure she could hear my heart beating. I told her I just felt the Lord leading me to stop and meet her, and I wanted to leave a gift with her. In spite of hearing a stranger say God told her to come see her, she was cordial. She told me something about going to a church that meets under some bridge. I just didn't have the stamina to pursue that, so I handed her the bag of food and said, "Everyone has to eat. So take this and enjoy it." We said goodbye, and that was that. It wasn't a real uplifting experience except for the fact that I knew God led me there, and she'd been shown a kindness along with an invitation to church. Seed planted. Now it was up to God.

About a month or so later, I was attending a Bible study at church. Afterwards I started driving home; it was just near dusk. Once again, thoughts of the bar came to mind. I wanted to invite the owner to come to our women's Bible study with me sometime. Would I stop in on the way home? Should I? Would it be too dark, and I'd be joining the Tuesday night crowd? I had to make a decision. As I drove along, I prayed, asking the Lord to give me wisdom and clarity about whether to do this thing or not. There went my heart again—beating like I was running a marathon! I could see the bar just up ahead, and I hadn't decided yet. As I neared the gravel drive, I swerved in and parked breathlessly. I knew not to falter because I'd turn around and go home. I pretended to be confident and walked right into the bar.

There were several patrons already enjoying a cold one, and I was quickly spotted by all of them, including the bartender. I had not been in a bar in probably thirty years, and this was not a comfortable feeling. But I walked over to the bartender and asked for the lady who was the owner. I was told she was not there and would be late coming back. So I coolly fumbled through my purse, retrieving a piece of paper with the calmest of hand (please note that this in itself was a miracle, as I have hands that tremble). I wrote her a personal note saying that I'd come by to see her and explaining why I had come. While I was writing, I heard vulgar remarks in the background from not one but several men. I acted as if I heard those remarks every day of my life. I asked the bartender to please give her my note when she returned. That I was inviting her to my church for a Bible study and was sorry I missed her. On my way out of the cave, I heard a man who was near the door and sitting alone say, "God bless you."

My husband was less than thrilled by that day's escapades, but he let it go as I assured him that God wouldn't let anything happen to me if I was doing what He wanted me to do. To this day, I don't know what impact if any all this had on the owner or the people there at the bar. All I know is that I followed God's leading. Obedience can be difficult. This was not easy to do, but I knew that God was with me, and He'd provide the courage I needed and would give power to my frail words. I pray that someone felt God's tug on their heart to know Him and follow Him. I'll never know. But one day. . . .

Witnessing to the Witnesses

> *The Holy Spirit will give you the words to say at the moment when you need them. (Luke 12:12 VOICE)*

Knowing this scripture we just read, why is it so difficult to open our mouths and speak for the Lord? Then, even when I get my mouth to open, my legs turn to jello! Such is the humanness of man.

If I could choose which of my many shortcomings and afflictions could be blotted out, I'd choose nervousness. I know scripture says, "[W]hen I am weak, then I am strong" (1 Cor.

12:10). I know that the Lord is with me always, and I know He is my strength and my mighty fortress. Even to the point that the Lord God Himself will actually put powerful words in my mouth at the appointed time! Yet I was created part jellyfish, it seems. I also wonder why the Lord has chosen me, Miss Jellyfish, to do such difficult things. Things that require confidence and a strong constitution. As I write this, I already know the answer, so I might as well accept God's will and get on with it. God wants to use me for His glory and His purpose. End of discussion.

We have to applaud the Jehovah Witnesses for their dedication to spreading what they believe. However, what they believe is false and is sin in the sight of the Lord. If we could combine the backbone of the Witnesses with the truth of God, we'd have a winning combination. But I am trying to do my part in taking a stand for truth no matter how hard or embarrassing or awkward it may be. God gave His best for me, and I am committed to giving Him my best in return.

I've actually known Christians who took some pride in the way they "handled" the Witnesses that came to their door. They bragged on their shortness with them, telling them to not come back again. They've shown anger in their faces. They have no place in their hearts for the Witnesses. Yet the Bible tells us that "such were some of you" (1 Cor. 6:11 ESV). We were all lost once, but we've been found only as we repented and turned over our lives to Jesus. So how can we be so rude to people whose eyes have been blinded spiritually by Satan as the Bible says? Jesus said He associated with the sinners because "it is not those who are healthy who need a physician but those who are sick. [He] did not come to call the righteous but sinners" (Mark 2:17 NASB).

I've been blessed to have had conversations, sort of, with Jehovah Witnesses. First, they do not want to hear what you have to say. And if they do let you speak, be prepared to hear an argument, said with all kindness, about what you just said. I prefer to shoot all my bullets at once and quickly, with a smile on my face, bid them a very nice day and goodbye. But I cannot dismiss the fact that the Lord Himself has just sent two lost souls to my front door. All I have to do is open it.

On a couple of occasions I met Witnesses where we lived on seven acres out in the country. I am a retired seamstress, and my shop was located a brisk walk from the house. It's a long way to run from the outbuildings to the house without being seen whenever a car has turned into your long gravel drive. So instead of trying to slink like a panther unseen to the house, I'd instead have a short but intense prayer with the Lord, straighten my back, and go out to meet them. I listened to two women once. Witnesses do not believe in the Holy Spirit as God or in the Trinity for that matter. Or that Jesus is God. Shall I go on? With jello legs, I put my arms across both of their shoulders and walked them out toward their car. I said that if they believed in God, then they should pray and ask Him to reveal to them whether they were believing truth or not. I said, "If you want to be sure, you should ask Him in prayer and wait for His answer." I told them that I loved them, and I wished them a good day. It wasn't perfect, but it was the best I could do. And I have to trust that God will do the rest.

Once a young Witness named Micah came to my front door out in the country. I didn't invite him in but asked him to please wait until I returned. I found a Bible that I intended ahead of time to give away. I went back to the door breathless—not because I ran but because my heart was beating so fast. Nerves! Yet I went on. I told Micah that God gave him a brain so that he could think for himself. I offered him my Bible, which he initially refused. Jehovah Witnesses will not read another person's Bible because they have a different version. Their Bible has been altered to say what men of this day want it to say. For instance, John 1:1 (CSB) tells us that "[i]n the beginning was the Word, and the Word was with God, and the Word was God." In their Bibles, it simply says the Word was *a god*. They refer to Jesus Christ, the name above all names, as *a* god. I kept insisting that Micah take the Bible and read it whenever he was alone, away from others who didn't want him to read it. He reluctantly took it. The adults waiting for him in the car probably confiscated it, but at least I did my part. And hopefully I put a grain of doubt in Micah's heart that maybe he didn't know everything about God. Acts 1:8 (NIV) says, "But you will receive power when the Holy Spirit comes on you, and you will be my witnesses in Jerusalem and in all Judea and Samaria and to the ends of the earth."

My husband took up the gauntlet of witnessing to the Witnesses too. I am always amazed at the calmness he displays, but he insists that he's done a poor job. I don't believe that. He has gone riding on his bike in the neighborhood—at age seventy, mind you—and has stopped and talked to Witnesses who were on their way to someone else's house. They just don't know what to make of that old Christian guy with gray hair and a helmet stopping to witness to them!

Several years back, I became so incredibly burdened for the children who were being raised in this false religion. That's what put me into action. I sat down at the desk and wrote down as many addresses as I could find of Jehovah Witness places of worship in my town and the surrounding areas. I wrote a simple but heartfelt letter to the pastors of each of these churches. I explained the gospel to them as the Bible accurately portrays it. I told them how wrong it was to think they can alter the words of the Bible according to their ideas. I explained how Jesus is God and that we don't have to be able to understand or fully comprehend the Holy Spirit to accept Him by faith.

There was a large Jehovah Witness church nearby that was next door to a small strip shopping center. For a while, because the burden was still on my heart for these people, I'd park in the shopping center parking lot so that I could see the church, and I'd pray with tears streaming from my eyes for the pastor and every congregant and child. Only the Lord knows what His Spirit did to their hearts. I'm a poor and impatient seed planter. I am only now learning how to fully trust God with the harvest, the outcome. I have been robbing myself of the joy of simply *belonging to God* by staying in a state of mourning for all the lost people I know. That's wrong because it is God and God alone who does the saving!

I was punishing myself needlessly. Of course it is His will that all be saved. Second Peter 3:9 (KJV) says, "The Lord is not slack concerning His promise, as some men count slackness; but is long suffering toward us, not willing that any should perish, but that all should come to repentance." I'm still a work in progress. So I need to remember that the battle is the Lord's, not mine.

EXAMINE YOURSELF

Have you ever had the opportunity to tell someone about Jesus? What did you do with that opportunity?

Does the thought of where they'll spend eternity ever enter your mind?

Who first told you about the Lord? How would your life have been different if they hadn't?

Do unbelievers anger you because of their behavior? Consider this—how else is a lost person to act except lost?

Does the thought of a loved one's passing cause you to have mental images of them talking to Jesus in heaven, or have you no thoughts at all?

Ask yourself these hard questions and consider if you really understand that death means hell for the unsaved. But to be absent from the body, for the believer, is to be present with the Lord. Is this your honest belief?

Chapter 12

END TIMES

And this gospel of the kingdom will be preached in the whole world as a testimony to all nations, and then the end will come.
—Matt. 24:14 (NIV)

When I was a teenager, I'd be at church because it was somewhere I was allowed to drive. I was mostly an unwilling participant, attending worship because, if you remember reading my testimony earlier, I only *thought* I was saved at age thirteen. Not until much later did I see when my salvation experience was genuine, which was more like when I was twenty-three years old. This is how and why I was so uncomfortable at church any time there was a message on the Rapture, End Times, or the Second Coming. Most times I wanted to crawl under a piece of furniture and hide until it was over, but the balcony seats provided no safe haven for me. So I would quietly get up out of my seat at the first of the message and stay in the women's restroom until time for the invitation. I did not want to hear any of those scary things! At least to me, they were scary because I just didn't understand. Especially being a lost person, I couldn't begin to grasp what was to be spiritually understood. So off to the restroom I'd go.

I know I'm not alone in that fear. Fear of the unknown will push people to do crazy things, like loitering in the women's restroom for forty-five minutes. To read the book of Revelation or to hear a well-prepared message on the End Times is downright frightening to anyone who doesn't know Jesus. Even Christians hear things from the Bible that are hard to wrap our minds around, but if we know Jesus, our take away from the message that was preached should be that our heavenly Father loves us and knows His children. Christians these days are trying to be patient as we excitedly await the Rapture. We are tired of this sin-sick world, and we long to go home where Jesus is. A true believer prays for Christ to come take His church home now. We know that He will take care of us even in the middle of end time chaos. We understand our personal end time will result with us being in heaven for all eternity, living in the joy of being with Jesus. So having a confidence in who our Father is and who we are in Him will always, without exception, smooth our ruffled feathers when we hear about unimaginable things to come—like the dragon, the false prophet, and the Antichrist. God has promised to never leave us or forsake us, and that's a promise we can take to the bank.

What is your personal reaction whenever you listen to sermons about End Times? Do you squirm like I did as a teenager? Or do you just turn off the television if it makes you uncomfortable? When we understand that the events in this world are unfolding exactly according to God's plan in His perfect timing, we can have a peace about us that the world knows nothing about. Of course, we don't look forward to persecution, economic collapse, wars, and destruction any more than the next man. But this is our hope—as we study the Bible, we learn that these things are to be expected but that the church, the Christians in the world, will be taken up out of this world before the awfulness and terror-filled part of the Tribulation begins. We believe the Bible, so we have faith in a better future.

Hebrews 11:1 says, "Faith shows the reality of what we hope for; it is the evidence of things we cannot see."

We cannot pretend to have faith in God if all our invested monies suddenly disappear. We cannot pretend to have faith if our jobs are taken away. We cannot pretend to have faith when inflation and natural disasters cause us to not be able to get food. These are times that we will need to have an *authentic faith* in Jesus Christ to be able to withstand the coming tide. As sin and evil advance in our world, so will fear and depression, suicide and hatred. These are symptoms of a world that has no hope. But God's promise of forgiveness of sin, salvation, and hope for an eternity in heaven is available to anyone at any time. If your heart is racing reading my mediocre descriptions of what is to come, then take this moment to ask God, in repentance, to save you. And He will! His Holy Spirit will be given to you. You'll receive a supernatural peace and hope for a future in heaven that can only be attributed to God and His great love for you.

> God's promise of forgiveness of sin, salvation, and hope for an eternity in heaven is available to anyone at any time.

Let me share an illustration I heard many years ago from a missionary who was visiting our church. It's such an accurate depiction of what we will be witnessing as time unfolds toward the end. I share this as a hope for those who can't see God intervening in the crime, hatred, and collapsing foundations that are around us.

The missionary told of something he witnessed that had tremendous strength and caused total destruction. He described the day that he heard a commotion in one of the jungle villages in Africa where he was living. It seems a mighty python had slithered its way inside one of the thatched huts belonging to a native family. So the owner pulled out a machete and with great force hacked off the head of the huge snake. Upon the delivery of this strike, the python began to thrash about with ferocious strength, ripping down the walls of the hut. Everything inside the hut was being destroyed and smashed and broken beyond recognition.

How could this happen when it had no head? It's a fact that a snake can survive twenty to forty-five minutes without a head, as its body still writhes about frantically. But eventually death comes.

The missionary explained that as the end nears for our world, things will get worse and worse as Satan thrashes about, destroying everything in his path because he knows his time is short. The Bible tells us that Satan has already lost the battle even while he's busy destroying. So in our last days on earth, we can expect Satan, whose head essentially has been severed, to violently work at using what time he has left to destroy what he can. But, praise God, his end is also coming! So when we see the awfulness of what's going on around us, take a moment to realize Satan is doing his last-minute thrashing before he dies. That kind of hope will help us live out each day, knowing that although life has become hellish, Satan's time is getting short, and our suffering is temporary.

Here is a sad fact. It is those who are not Christians who are living each day as if time is never going to end. They live today the same as yesterday with no thought of tomorrow. They may see the world going up in smoke but have become so accustomed to evil they're blind to what's happening around them. Just a couple of days ago, I was driving down the highway through our town and witnessed something that is seldom seen these day—a street preacher! It was wonderful to see this man standing boldly on the corner of the intersection with a Bible open in hand and his face turned to the heavens proclaiming the gospel of Jesus Christ! I couldn't help but smile, and I thought of the Apostle Paul and others who were so courageous in their preaching.

I looked around to see how others were responding. Most were not even giving him a glance, but some were staring. I wondered if any were really hearing. I wondered who went home that day with a godly seed planted in their heart. Could God use this bellowing street preacher to reach someone for Christ? God tells us in Isaiah 55:10-11, "The rain and snow come down from the heavens and stay on the ground to water the earth. They cause the grain to grow, producing seed for the farmer and bread for the hungry. It is the same with my Word. I send it out, and it always produces fruit. It will accomplish all I want it to, and it will prosper everywhere I send it."

EXAMINE YOURSELF

What would your reaction be if you saw someone preaching boldly from the Bible on a street corner? Would you criticize him? Would you feel insulted or embarrassed? Or would you be proud for this individual, wishing you had the same kind of courage, praying that someone would be saved through the sharing of God's Word?

Do you become fearful hearing how prophesies are being fulfilled and the end is coming closer?

Do you rest in God's amazing strength and comfort and strive to live for Christ even when dark days come?

Do you believe the Bible when He tells us Jesus Christ has already won the battle?

Chapter 13

CONCLUSION

We must now ask ourselves, as we have unearthed the true meaning of frequently heard words and statements of the Christian faith, *are we genuinely saved?* How will we now answer the question, "I believe in God, so I'm saved, right?" It's my sincere prayer that our understanding of "believing in God" has been challenged and that we've had questions answered. Or are we still staking our eternal future on erroneous or wishful thinking on a "hope so" mindset? Has Satan so cleverly tricked us into a false type of belief? Are we *sure* that we can be found in Christ?

Alistair Begg makes this true observation concerning punishment we deserve from God in contrast to kindness we do not deserve. He said, "Do you remember when your father or mother, when you deserved a significant reinforcement of the principals of parental jurisdiction, they showed kindness to you? Oh, those tears were the biggest tears on my pillow! Far bigger than the tears that emerged from the sting in my tail. That, I knew I deserved. This kindness, I did not deserve."[26] As Ephesians

---

26. Alistair Begg, "Saved by Grace" audio message (ID:3167), truthforlife.org, May 1, 2016.

3:18 pleads from the heart of Paul, "And may you have the power to understand, as all God's people should, how wide, how long, how high, and how deep His love is." When Jesus suffered his violent death on the cross, He had you personally on His mind. If you've ever doubted God's love for you, *just look at the cross!* It was for *you* that He stayed on the cross. Jesus absorbed God's wrath that was meant for us. And the moment we choose to follow Jesus in repentance and obedience, God Himself places Christ's robe of righteousness across our shoulders and takes on Himself all the filthy sin we once owned. Never have we been so gloriously loved! Such a wonderful testimony of that love is the blood of Christ. Why would we not long to surrender our entire selves to such love?

> If you've ever doubted God's love for you, *just look at the cross!* It was for *you* that He stayed on the cross.

Romans 2:4 tenderly tells us, "Don't you see how wonderfully kind, tolerant, and patient God is with you? Does this mean nothing to you? Can't you see that His kindness is intended to turn you from your sin?"

> Anyone who might feel reluctant to surrender his will to the will of another should remember Jesus' words, "Whosoever committeth sin is the servant of sin" (John 8:34 KJV). We must of necessity be servant to someone, either to God or to sin. The sinner prides himself on his independence, completely overlooking the fact that he is the weak slave of the sins that rule his members. The man who surrenders to Christ exchanges a cruel slave driver for a kind and gentle Master whose yoke is easy and whose burden is light.[27]

As you complete the reading of this book, are you seeing yourself through different eyes? Has God shown you areas of

---

27. A. W. Tozer, *The Pursuit of God*, from "The Essential Tozer Collection," compiled and edited by James L. Snyder (Minneapolis, MN: Bethany House, a division of Baker Publishing Group, 2017)

CONCLUSION

your life that may not be genuine? If He has, how wonderful! This underscores the fact that God is and probably has been trying to reach you to speak to your heart. Scripture tells us that no man seeks God. That's because, as has been mentioned before, until we see our sin, we won't even see our need for a Savior. God is relentless in His loving pursuit of you and desires to have a true relationship with you. His mercy has been poured out on you as you have awakened each morning, giving you yet another day to humbly submit your life, *every part of it*, and your heart to His lordship. He died for you. Will you now choose to live authentically for Him?

> *Father God, it is my humble plea that You will, through your amazing grace and unending mercy, open the eyes of those who have gone through life with their spiritual eyes closed to the truth of Your Word. Let the scales fall from their eyes as the evil one seeks to devour them through his deceit. Help each one to take time to examine their heart to see whether they are of the household of faith. Show them, as they search for the truth about their belief, that only a fully surrendered life devoted to following the One who died for them will be acceptable in God's sight. Show them that we must die to ourselves, removing ourselves from the throne of our hearts. Help them realize that only through forgiveness that Christ alone can give will we be able to enjoy heaven with Jesus for all eternity. Open their minds to understanding the scripture that they have read in these pages, and cause those holy words to burn into their very souls, convicting them, changing them into the new creations in Christ that is promised to us all who repent and follow our Lord Jesus Christ. We thank You for Your love, Your sacrifice, and the eternal hope You are to us. Forgive us all where we fail You every day. We come humbly, asking for Your Holy Spirit to change our lives, our minds, our eternity. For it is in the precious name of Jesus Christ, our Savior, I pray. Amen.*

AFTERWORD: THE ROAD TO SALVATION

You are probably familiar with what is called the Roman Road. These are several scripture verses from the book of Romans in the New Testament that explain step by step the way to salvation, almost as if you're walking down a road, reading signposts along the way. It might be helpful to write the location of these verses on the inside cover of your Bible or mark them by numbering them in their specific order in the book of Romans. Remember what you have learned in this book about the kind of belief that leads to true salvation.

> *For everyone has sinned; we all fall short of God's glorious standard. (Rom. 3:23)*
>
> *For the wages of sin is death, but the free gift of God is eternal life through Jesus Christ our Lord. (Rom. 6:23)*
>
> *For everyone who calls on the name of the Lord will be saved. (Rom. 10:13)*
>
> *But God showed His great love for us by sending Christ to die for us while we were still sinners. (Rom. 5:8)*
>
> *So now there is no condemnation for those who belong to Christ Jesus. (Rom. 8:1)*
>
> *If you confess with your mouth that Jesus is Lord and believe in your heart that God raised Him from the dead, you will be saved. For it is by believing in your heart that you are made right with God, and it is by confessing with your mouth that you are saved. (Rom. 10:9-10)*

AFTERWORD: THE ROAD TO SALVATION

If you are seeing yourself right now as a sinner in need of Christ's forgiveness, you are blessed! Blessed because you have finally come to the end of yourself—you see your hopelessness and wretchedness and are now seeking what only Christ can offer: eternal life! Simply talk to God in a private place, expressing your desire to belong to Him. Agree with God that you are a sinner. Prayer is no more than talking personally and candidly to God, spilling your heart to Him just as you would your own father. Then, in obedience to Him, repent of your sin, turn fully to Him, commit your life to following His commands, live your life in a way that is pleasing to Him. He's now your King! Your Father! Your Savior! God will freely, joyfully, and immediately give you His forgiveness and His Holy Spirit as well. From this point on, when God sees you, He will not see your sins but only the righteousness of His Son, Jesus, on your life.

The Holy Spirit is the third Person of the Trinity, which is God the Father, God the Son, and God the Holy Spirit. While God is Spirit and seated on His throne in heaven, Jesus Christ is in His glorified body, seated at the right hand of His Father in heaven. God gave His children the amazing gift of His Holy Spirit that lives inside all who are saved here on earth to be our protector, provider, and defender. God gave Him to us to be our compass, to lead us in decision-making, to give us wise counsel, to remind us of His Word, to comfort us when we are alone or afraid, to convict us when we sin or are tempted to sin. He is God living in us! Yes, this is a supernatural occurrence, and your life will never be the same as you navigate the harsh realities this world offers—but with the complete assurance that God is with you and will never leave you or forsake you and that your real home is in heaven. Therefore live each day strengthened in the knowledge that we are just travelers for now in a foreign land and that heaven is our forever home.

Printed in the USA
CPSIA information can be obtained
at www.ICGtesting.com
JSHW012032090924
69407JS00008B/93